This book is dedicated to the memory of my parents,
Bruce and Elfarata Treble

BILL TREBLE

GETTING INTO THE BIDDING

A BRIDGE TOOLKIT

Master Point Press • Toronto, Canada

Master Point Press
331 Douglas Ave.
Toronto, Ontario, Canada
M5M 1H2 (416)781-0351
info@masterpointpress.com
Websites: www.masterpointpress.com
           www.teachbridge.com
           www.bridgeblogging.com
           www.ebooksbridge.com

Library and Archives Canada Cataloguing in Publication

Treble, Bill
    Getting into the bidding : a bridge toolkit / Bill Treble.

Issued also in electronic formats.
ISBN 978-1-897106-85-3

    1. Contract bridge--Bidding. I. Title.

GV1282.4.T74 2012   795.41'52   C2011-908639-5

We acknowledge the financial support of the Government of Canada through the Book Publishing Industry Development Program (BPIDP) for our publishing activities.

Editor   Ray Lee
Copy editor/interior format   Sally Sparrow
Cover and interior design   Olena S. Sullivan/New Mediatrix

1 2 3 4 5 6 7   16 15 14 13 12

PRINTED IN CANADA

Contents

INTRODUCTION

When I first started to play bridge, most of the books and publications dealt with auctions where your side had a free run with no interference. Whether you played Standard American or one of the more elaborate systems popularized overseas, the focus was on reaching the best contract. Takeout and negative doubles got some ink, but overcalls in those days were near-opening bids in high-card strength, and partner was expected to bid accordingly.

For several reasons, however, people began to make overcalls more frequently. There was a growing recognition that excellent shape is just as important as points in deciding whether to compete. Soon, some players abandoned the idea of insisting on "the goods" for a direct overcall, hoping for a chance to balance later with hands that weren't quite so robust. Instead, they'd display a willingness to get involved right away if the level was convenient, as opposed to waiting for the perfect hand to take direct action.

The widening of the overcall range, combined with a move towards a friskier preempting style, vaulted competitive bidding to the forefront rather than merely being an afterthought. A healthy amount of discussion was needed if both the opening and interfering sides were to keep a sure footing.

The nature of bridge literature changed in tandem, with a proliferation of books devoted to specific aspects of the topic. For example, Mike Lawrence has written on overcalling and balancing, and both Larry Cohen and Andrew Robson have dealt with higher-level battles. What seems to be lacking so far is a one-stop shopping experience that covers the entire realm in a fair amount of detail but at a pace that won't cause the reader to experience a sense of overload.

This book is intended to build a foundation that will enable you to succeed in the hurly-burly of the contested auction. It naturally divides into three stages. In Chapters 1 to 4, we look at competitive actions that occur immediately after the opening bid or relatively early in the bidding. Moving on to Chapters 5 to 7, we find out about several ways to compete over their 1NT opening and also talk about how to claim your fair share of the turf as the bidding continues, both in low-level auctions and way up there in the stratosphere. At this point, you are in a good position to flourish if you have digested the contents sufficiently. If you happen to be in a regular, serious partnership with higher aspirations, Chapters 8 and 9 contain lots of good reference material for arriving at firm understandings. There are quiz hands throughout, and an entire chapter of them to wrap things up.

In the thirty-plus years that I've played bridge, I've met many wonderful and interesting people who have shared their insights and experience with me. Much of their advice is included in these pages. For example, Colin Ward, who always has a quip for any occasion, came up with the gem that "The only effective defense to a preempt is an overbid." Well, maybe.

I'd like to mention three people especially, with all of whom I've had long-standing partnerships. One is Tom Butterworth, who took me on when he was one of the top players in our area and I still had some rough edges on my game. He was not only a wellspring of knowledge that benefited me greatly, but his temperament, sportsmanship and genuine friendliness towards everyone at the table was a shining example for us all. Dave McLellan was an excellent match for me in plunging into an abundance of intricate bidding techniques. Watching him play, I saw his intensity and desire to scale the heights, and as a declarer, he was able to work out the layout of just about every hand he played. Finally, there is my wife Sue, who has not only enriched my life in every way imaginable, but is a walking advertisement for having no fear at the bridge table. Some years ago, when I kept rambling on about doing a book on competitive bidding, she finally had enough of it and said, "Well, when are you going to stop talking about it and get cracking?" She always gives me a nudge and a wakeup call when I sorely need it. Love ya, Sue.

CHAPTER 1

PRINCIPLES OF COMPETING AND BASIC TOOLS

Effective bidding in contested auctions is a vital part of winning bridge, and its importance cannot be stressed highly enough. I often play bridge on the internet, and I did a study of some recent sessions. Here are the statistics:

Tournament #	Unobstructed Auctions	Both Sides Bidding
1	5	7
2	3	9
3	5	5
4	5	7
5	6	6
6	5	7
Total	29	41

Over the course of six sessions, then, competitive auctions represented almost 60% of the deals played. Because a lot of current theory and many of the books you read now emphasize an 'in your face' style of interfering with the opponents, the bidding landscape has changed significantly over the course of the last 10-20 years. To take one example, a strong notrump opening would usually buy the contract in a bygone era. Not so anymore. From personal experience, I can tell you that more often than not the opponents are butting in over our 1NT openings with some kind of one- or two-suited overcall.

You can get mildly annoyed at these tactics, or even downright upset, but it's a fact of life that isn't going to change. Moreover, to operate effectively in this highly-charged environment, you also have to be willing to get your own feet wet in the bidding, using moderately aggressive but sensible parameters. This book is intended to build a complete framework, in stages, whereby you'll be able to develop the tools needed to produce good results in auctions where both sides are vying for the contract. To reach this goal, I'll lay out a solid foundation, while at the same time dispensing with some widely-held misconceptions about competitive bidding. The main themes I'll be discussing in this chapter are:

- Understanding what distributional type of hand you have, and using that to assist you in close decisions as to whether to get involved in the bidding.
- The 'loose' and 'classic' way of playing takeout doubles, and a recommendation on which of the two styles to adopt.
- Overcalls. I'll describe the goals of overcalling, that two of three criteria should always be met, and how the level of the bidding affects what you need for an overcall. I'll also talk about how to proceed when partner makes an overcall.
- Deciding, when RHO opens, whether your hand is worth one or two actions. This will often assist you in determining what your initial salvo is going to be.
- Reopening doubles in passout seat and negative doubles. Why you have to have firm understandings in place to get to the right spot.

Distributional Types

When you are opening the bidding, the main emphasis is placed on high-card points. Extra length in suits also has some worth, no doubt about it. However, in a 'free run' auction, the goal is to find a game contract, which is going to require a certain number of high-card points, although distributional assets may be of some help.

At least to some extent, the opposite is the case in a competitive auction. Even a respectable number of high-card points may not count for much if you don't have the power of long suits (for an overcall) or short suits (for a takeout double) to back it up. If you have a good hand and RHO opens, it's anyone's guess as to which side has the majority of the high cards. That being the case, some nice distributional features are advisable to provide a safety net if your side is outgunned pointwise.

This table classifies the most common hand patterns:

Balanced	Mildly Unbalanced	Unbalanced	Wildly Unbalanced
4333	5422	4441	7321
4432	6322	5431	7330
5332		5521	6511
		5530	6520
		6331	any 6-6 shape
			8+ card suit

When an opponent has opened, it is extremely risky to jump into the bidding with one of the balanced distributions, particularly the 4333 hand type. You need a full opening bid with the hands in this group to consider acting, the only exception being the 5332 hand, and then only if you can bid your long suit at the one-level.

The mildly unbalanced hands have more upside for competing, and you can entertain the thought with marginally less than an opening bid.

The same guidelines apply for a hand that qualifies as unbalanced, especially with the more extreme shapes of 5521, 5530 and 6331, unless they've bid one of your suits. With 5431 you'd lean towards bidding, and with 4441 you can make a takeout double if they've opened your short suit.

With the severely unbalanced hands, your default position should be making some kind of bid, unless you have nothing to speak of in high-card points.

The trend, however, is that if you're stuck in the left-hand column with your distribution, you need a goodly combination of pictures on your cards to set you in motion. As you move across the spectrum and nearer to the right-hand column, the increased likelihood of a playable fit should get the competitive juices flowing.

THE 'DEATH HOLDING'

You may or may not have heard this curious expression used in regards to bridge. It's used to describe the cards you have in the suit an opponent has bid.

Suppose they have opened with 1♠ and you have five or more cards in one of the other suits with a decent hand. Let's examine some possible spade holdings for you and assess them:

x x or x   Not bad. You can ruff if they keep playing the suit.

x x x x   The downside is that you have quite a few losers in their suit. The possible bright spot is that partner might not have a lot of them and *if* he has a fit with your long suit, you should have the capability of trumping some of your low cards in dummy.

x x x or Q x x	The absolute pits — this is the 'death holding'. Whereas on the first two layouts you might have two or fewer losers, here there is the very real chance of having three, either in top tricks or via the third round being trumped by opener's partner.

If you happen to be on the edge as to whether to enter the fray or not, one of the deciding considerations should be your holding in the enemy suit. Whereas length or shortness can be arguments in favor of bidding, the three-card 'death holding' should be a deterrent.

Losing Trick Count (LTC): Use this tool with care

This section is for those of you that have heard the expression 'losing trick count' bandied about and are considering using it as a method of evaluating the potential of your hand.

The 'standard' losing trick count (LTC) assigns a loser for every one of the top three cards (ace, king or queen) that you are missing in a suit. Moreover, you do *not* count a loser for the fourth and subsequent cards in a suit. To see how this works, look at the following holdings and apply the formula to them:

a) A K 6   b) K J 3   c) A Q 9 5   d) J 10 7 2

Example (a) has one loser, as you have three cards and are missing one of the top three honors. In example (b), you are missing the ace and queen of the suit and will assign yourself a loser for each of them. Ergo, two losers. In example (c), you have one loser. How do we arrive at that number? You are missing the king, so give yourself one loser there. What about the fourth card? LTC assumes that it will establish through length and so does not consider it to be a loser. Finally, in example (d), you have three losers as you are missing the ace, king and queen of the suit. However, once again, you do not consider the fourth card to be a loser.

The problem with hand evaluation tools such as LTC is that they tend to be relied upon as gospel, whereas any such aid must be utilized with a certain degree of judgment. The word 'rule' tends to set you on auto-pilot and creates the dangerous impression that you merely apply the formula and don't have to engage in a deeper level of thinking. Better words would be 'principle', 'guideline' or 'reference point'. These things are meant to supplement your own instincts and thought processes, not to replace them.

Let's go on to a couple of new examples where you should be applying some good old-fashioned common sense in the usage of the LTC:

a) A K 10 4   b) K Q 6 5   c) Q 6 3 2   d) Q J 9 8

LTC considers both (a) and (b) to be one-loser holdings, and just by looking at them, you know you'd prefer to have the AK10x. You will never lose more than two tricks, and your fourth card will probably grow up because you have the ten as a 'kicker'. You can also play the top winners out of your hand if need be. With the KQxx, you need to reach dummy to play the suit to best advantage, and might still need the ace favorably placed *and* a 3-3 split to hold yourself to one loser.

Similarly, holding (d) is clearly better than (c) because of the fillers you have with the nine and eight of the suit. You'll never lose more than three tricks with the QJ98, and if you have sufficient entries to dummy, there is a fair chance to lose only two tricks even opposite three small. Not so with the Qxxx, as there's a very real chance of losing four tricks in the suit even if you can play it from dummy.

Losing Trick Count works best if a playable fit exists in one or more suits. The course of the bidding, however, is sometimes a warning not to rely too heavily on LTC. Here is an example from a recent event that illustrates this kind of pitfall. Non-vulnerable against vulnerable opponents, you hold:

♠x ♡Q J 9 x x ◇A K Q 10 9 x x ♣—

LHO	Partner	RHO	You
			1◇
2♣	pass	3NT	?

With this three-loser hand, you open 1◇ brimming with optimism, since if partner has a red-suit fit and at least a smattering of points, there will be a good chance of making game. At the next chance to bid, those hopes have been scattered to the wind. With LHO making a vulnerable two-level overcall and righty jumping to 3NT, partner rates to be virtually broke in high cards. There won't be a diamond fit, as RHO will have four or five to the jack for his 3NT bid. I don't think many people could resign themselves to passing, although it would have been right at the table. If you're going to bid, then with storm clouds looming on the horizon it's essential to choose the option with the least downside, and that would be 4◇, not 4♡. It turns out partner has two small hearts, a singleton diamond, and not much else — not a huge surprise given the bidding.

While Losing Trick Count has gained in popularity and has some value, it's a mere part of the entire picture, not the be-all and end-all of bidding. It is best taken with a grain of salt, and works most effectively when other aspects of your hand are factored into the total equation.

Takeout Doubles

Although most textbooks specify clear parameters for a takeout double, students and players who have just ventured into organized bridge find it hard to resist competing when they have 12 or more high-card points. They naturally feel the inclination to jump in since you are expected to open the bidding with similar values.

Accordingly, there are two distinct styles with respect to takeout doubles. They are:

Classical When the opponents bid first, a double shows at most two cards in their suit, at least three-card support for the other suits and preferably four-card support for any unbid major.

The only hands where the doubler would have more than two cards in the enemy suit are very strong ones. One example would be 17+ HCP with a five-card or longer suit, a hand that is too good for a mere overcall. The other is a balanced hand of 19+ HCP that is too strong for a 1NT overcall.

If partner is a passed hand and you are in the 14-15 HCP range with pure values (aces and kings), you might double with 4333 shape. However, if you are facing an unpassed partner, it's better to shy away from that kind of action.

The 'My Turn to Bid' Double

If you look at the ACBL convention card, under 'Special doubles', there is a box to tick off that states 'Min. Offshape TO'. That's for the people who tend to double an opening bid with most 12-15 point balanced hands regardless of the holdings in the unbid suits. It's somewhat of a misnomer in that the double is not specifically 'offshape', but rather that it *could* be.

Some players will blithely sail into the auction on any 12-14 HCP, claiming it as their prerogative, quite irked that RHO had the gall to open in front of them. However, when the opponents are into the auction first, the odds of game or slam have declined since you know where almost a third or even more of the high-card points are. You are on far more shaky ground in bidding now, and need your distribution to justify entering the auction. If there's a good chance of locating a fit, you should definitely get in there. Having a five- or six-card suit to overcall increases the likelihood of a playable contract. With a 12-15 point balanced hand, you might not have any such safe harbor and may well be headed for a minus, perhaps a disastrous one if your LHO is loaded with most of the remaining high-card points.

It's for these reasons that I'm an advocate of the classic takeout double. The best ones are where you have a singleton or void in RHO's suit and at least four-card support for everything else. If you have a 4432 hand pattern, your doubleton should be in their suit, again meeting the requirements for a takeout double.

Why is it so important to have these stringent requirements for a takeout double? It's a case of less being more. You might not get into as many auctions with the classic takeout doubles, but when your side does, it will be able to compete far more effectively. Having to pass with opening values at the start does not preclude a later entry into the bidding, as we'll see later on.

Before moving on to an example, let's get acquainted with some terminology. Opener's partner is the **responder**, as we all know. The partner of a takeout doubler or overcaller has a name too — the **advancer**. With the takeout double especially, that person *advances* the double to what should be the best trump fit for their side.

Here's a typical situation for advancer to deal with. Your hand is:

♠ A 7 6   ♡ Q 5   ◇ 10 8 4   ♣ Q 9 7 5 3

Now we have this start to the bidding — they're vulnerable and you aren't:

LHO	Partner	RHO	You
1♠	dbl	2♠	?

Partner clearly doesn't have that many of their spades. It's possible 3♣ could make and even if it doesn't, -50 could be a decent result if they have +110 their way for 2♠ making. It would seem right, then, to bid, and if partner has a reasonable facsimile of a takeout double, like:

♠ 5 3   ♡ A J 10 2   ◇ A 9 6 4   ♣ K J 8

your result will be jim-dandy: you make at least +110 your way regardless of what they lead, as dummy's hearts will enable you to pitch losers. Alas, partner slaps down this as your reward:

♠ K Q   ♡ A 10 7 2   ◇ K 9 5 3 2   ♣ J 8

This hand isn't quite as suitable, and 3♣ could well go minus with 2♠ a non-make for them. Partner defends himself in a familiar refrain, 'Well, I had good support for two of the unbid suits but you had to go and bid the third one instead. I did have opening points, you know.'

So how should the last hand have proceeded? Should it have overcalled in diamonds instead? We'll revisit this particular hand later on in this chapter, and get to the correct solution in due time.

BIDDING OVER PARTNER'S TAKEOUT DOUBLE

Most introductory courses on bridge talk about what to do when partner makes a takeout double, but don't go into a whole lot of detail beyond a cursory reference. We'll try and flesh it out a bit in this section, using the following auction to illustrate:

LHO	Partner	RHO	You
1◇	dbl	pass	?

Since RHO has passed, you have to do *something*, even with a very bad hand. Your duty is to steer your side into the best spot, which is usually going to be one of the other three suits. You, the advancer, can select between the following options, depending on the shape and point count in your hand:

1♡/1♠/2♣   Any *non-jump* would show 0 to a bad 8 HCP and be your choice between the unbid suits the doubler has advertised. It's worth noting this will also apply to 2♣, in contrast to going to the two-level after an opening bid in an uncontested auction. Suppose your hand is:

♠76 ♡J9 ◇854 ♣K 10 7 6 5 3

You want to designate clubs as the trump suit, as partner will have at least three of them. It's really all that you're interested in, and partner should realize that since you haven't jumped, you may not have a whole lot of values.

1NT   Since you are bidding notrump opposite known shortness in partner's hand, you need a double stopper and a reasonable number of HCP as well — 8 to a bad 11 — for an adequate measure of safety in a notrump contract.

2♡/2♠/3♣   These jumps would all show a good 8 to a bad 11 HCP. For 3♣, which takes us to a higher level, it's best to have at least 9 HCP, settling for 2♣ with an 8-count.

2NT   A good 11 or 12 HCP, at least one stopper in the enemy suit and preferably two. Denies a four-card or longer major.

3NT	12 or more HCP, denies a four-card or longer major, should have diamonds well stopped.
2◊	The cuebid of the enemy suit shows 12+ HCP and is game-forcing if advancer is an unpassed hand. Typically it shows support for at least two suits and defers the selection of the trump suit to the doubler, at least for the time being. An example hand for a cuebid would be:

♠A 10 6 3 ♡Q 10 9 5 ◊7 4 ♣A Q 8

Rather than jump to game in a major and risk playing a 4-3 fit, cuebid and then raise whatever major the doubler then bids.

pass	See below.

Here's a hand that gives you a problem when partner makes a takeout double of your LHO's 1◊ opening:

♠K 9 7 ♡8 2 ◊7 6 5 4 2 ♣J 5 3

Ugh! Ugh! Triple Ugh! Now why did partner have to go and make a takeout double? Most people who face this quandary either bid 1NT over the double or pass, since they have no four-card or longer suit. Unfortunately, neither of those choices is a viable option. The opponents will surely be making 1◊, likely with overtricks, so sitting for the double won't result in a good score. You, on the other hand, won't have any chance of making 1NT opposite a minimum takeout double and may well get doubled there for penalties, so that bid is equally fruitless.

Okay, Einstein, you might ask, what would *you* do? Well, I'd hold my nose and bid 1♠. Partner asked me to choose from the other three suits, and that's about the best I can do. Look at it this way: you are probably destined for a minus on this hand, and you want it to be a flesh wound rather than a massive hemorrhage. At least the doubler will realize that you have 0 to a bad 8 HCP when you bid 1♠, and is going to pass with a minimum hand. The end result is that you'll be in a 4-3 fit at the one-level, and while it won't be great, it won't be as tragic as leaving in the double or bidding 1NT.

♠A 7 6 ♡Q 5 ◊K J 10 9 6 ♣9 7 4

This is the hand on which you would pass a takeout double of 1◊, with a strong five-card or longer holding in their suit and some values on the side.

You expect to beat 1◇ doubled at least two, maybe three tricks, and you may not have a game your way. By the way, whenever you leave in a low-level takeout double for penalties, partner should lead a trump — your pass is saying you probably have better trumps than they do.

ADVANCING A TAKEOUT DOUBLE WHEN RHO BIDS

In many ways, when RHO bids over partner's takeout double it is an advantage for your side. For one thing, you are off the hook — you don't have to bid when you have 0-5 HCP or even a lousy 6-count. However, you should be interested in competing for the partscore if you have 7 or more HCP. Moreover, you should be perfectly willing to come in with a four-card suit. Playing classic takeout doubles, partner will usually have four of them for you, especially if it's an unbid major. He or she will always have at least three-card support. If you compete without jumping, that shows 7-9 points, and if you jump one level, you need a very good 9 to 11 points.

LHO	Partner	RHO	You
1♣	dbl	1♠	?

♠ x x   ♡ A J x x   ◇ K x x   ♣ x x x x

Bid 2♡. Your side has at least half the deck in points and the doubler is presumed to have four-card support for the unbid major suits. You want to advertise to partner a smattering of values and length in hearts. Since you haven't jumped, he will assume 7-9 points.

♠ x x   ♡ A J 10 x x   ◇ J x x   ♣ A x x

Bid 3♡. This hand with 10 HCP is worth a more bullish action. Both 2♡ and 3♡ are 'free bids' by advancer, indicating some values. The difference is that 2♡ is merely vying for a partscore, whereas the jump to 3♡ strongly invites game.

♠ A J x   ♡ x x   ◇ Q J 9 x x   ♣ x x x

Bid 2◇. Even if partner only has three of them, you'll still have at least an eight-card fit. Don't fret about the 'death holding' in LHO's clubs — partner will have at most two of them since he's made a takeout double.

♠ J x ♡ A x x ◇ Q 9 x x ♣ Q J 10 x

Bid 1NT. Bidding 2◇ is also a possibility, but you have 10 HCP and your side will have both of their suits stopped. Are you worried about a spade lead? You shouldn't be. Remember, partner has made a takeout double and rates to have four of them.

STILL TAKEOUT OR NOT? A COUPLE OF EXAMPLES

A couple of auctions worth discussing for any partnership are:

LHO	Partner	RHO	You
		1♠	pass
1NT	dbl	pass	?

Most teachers will explain that a double is takeout if it meets two criteria: the first is that the contract is a partscore, and the second is that your side has not previously bid.

In this auction, the double is for takeout because it satisfies both conditions. Takeout of what? Spades, the only suit the opponents have bid.

LHO	Partner	RHO	You
1♠	dbl	2♠	pass
pass	dbl	pass	?

In this sequence, the second double is also for takeout, just as the first one was. The precept 'once a takeout double, always a takeout double' applies and the enemy contract is still a partscore. With his second action, partner will have a mighty fine hand, in the range of 17 or more HCP, as you might have very little and he is forcing the auction to the three-level.

Overcalling

DOWN-TO-EARTH OR WILD-AND-WOOLLY?

Like many bids, the overcall has been either watered-down or spruced-up in the last twenty-five years, depending on your viewpoint. It was once a near-cousin to an opening bid, usually 12 or more points. A 10-11 point hand would be acceptable at favorable vulnerability if you had a good suit and could make your overcall at the one-level.

Nowadays, overcalls have become somewhat more aggressive. I've seen them made on as little as 6 or 7 points and a half-decent suit. While this style definitely generates action, advancer might have a tough go of it with a wide (say 7-17) overcall range if the opponents contest the auction further. As a result it is tough to cope on a hand and auction like the following:

LHO	Partner	RHO	You
1♣	1◇	dbl	redbl
2♣	pass	pass	2◇
pass	pass	3♣	3◇
all pass			

♠A93 ♡AK83 ◇Q654 ♣86

You'd expect, with a full opening bid and good four-card support, that partner would have a decent play for 3◇. Not so in this case, as the 1◇ overcall was:

♠872 ♡J65 ◇AJ1087 ♣107

and 3◇ had five losers, while 3♣ was going down their way. It's not really good for partnership harmony when you lay down your gem of a hand only to have the contract fail miserably. Yet if we give partner 9 or 10 points with ♣Kx or ♣Ax instead of two small, 3◇ makes easily and 3NT would have a play as well.

There are two distinct breeds of overcalls. For now we'll focus on the **simple overcall**, where you introduce your suit at the cheapest level (e.g. 1♠ over their 1◇, or 2♡ over their 1♠). There is also the **jump overcall**, an example of which would be a bid of 2♠ after the opponents start with 1◇. We'll elaborate on them in greater detail in Chapter 2.

There are three potential benefits to your side for overcalling, which are:

- You may buy the contract.
- You can suggest a productive lead if they end up declaring the hand.
- It could have some preemptive effect, denying your LHO the space to make the bid he would otherwise have chosen.

The rule that I will be advocating is that even a one-level overcall should generally be 10 or more points, with only very few exceptions. You should never make a simple overcall with as few as 6 or 7 points. With a hand in the 8-9 range, it's acceptable to overcall at the one-level with a six-card or longer suit. With only a five-card suit, you should only overcall if it achieves at least two of the purposes described above. I'll look back to partner's hand for that 1◇ overall to show you what I mean:

♠ 8 7 2   ♡ J 6 5   ◇ A J 10 8 7   ♣ 10 7

This hand is balanced, which as we said at the beginning is one of the riskier patterns to interfere with. Besides, that, it only meets one of the objectives for competing: suggesting a lead for partner. There is little if any intent or ability to buy the contract, and a 1◇ overcall does not preclude LHO from responding in either major suit, so there is no preemptive effect. Now let's take a look at another hand, not a whole lot stronger, but with a few small improvements:

♠ A J 10 8 5   ♡ 9 6   ◇ Q 10 9 7   ♣ 6 4

We'll assume the same 1♣ opening on the right. This hand is mildly unbalanced, and that reduces the number of potential losers. More importantly, overcalling 1♠ now has two things going for it. It still has some lead-directing value, and takes away LHO's ability to mention either diamonds or hearts at the one-level. I wouldn't personally overcall 1♠ with this hand, but if someone elected to venture in at favorable vulnerability, I'd consider it aggressive but not totally outlandish.

Now, on to a couple more hands:

♠ Q J 10 7 4   ♡ 7 5   ◇ A 10 7 6   ♣ K 3

♠ A 9 5 4 2   ♡ K 9 6   ◇ J 5 3   ♣ Q 8

You can overcall 1♠ over 1♣ with the first of these hands at any vulnerability. It's mildly unbalanced, which is a plus, and the ♣K should be a trick as it sits behind the opening bidder.

The second hand is balanced, has a losing trick count of nine, and the quality of the long suit is mediocre. Only consider overcalling not vulnerable, and even then it's marginal at best.

Two-level overcalls should never be skimped on, as they are venturing to a more dangerous level. I would suggest these guidelines:

a) With 8 or fewer points, do not even dream of overcalling at the two-level. If you have a seven-card or longer suit, you could make a preemptive bid, but partner will expect a better hand if you make a simple overcall.

b) With 9-10 points, don't overcall at the two-level unless you are not vulnerable and have a six-card or longer suit, preferably with an unbalanced hand.

c) With 11-13 HCP, it's not a great idea to be overcalling at the two-level with a balanced hand unless your suit is good quality — at least AQJ9x. If you have a six-card or longer suit, or are 5-4 in two suits, bidding is much safer. Also remember that the 'death holding' in opener's suit is a warning sign that shouldn't be ignored.

d) With 14 or more points you should always be getting in there with a long suit, even if it's only a five-carder. If partner is relatively broke or there are foul splits, it might not turn out well, but that's life. It's hard to catch up later if you don't take action right off the bat.

With these guidelines in place, we can now use them to judge whether or not to make a two-level overcall in the following examples:

LHO	Partner	RHO	You
		1♠	?

♠ 8 7   ♡ A Q 10 7 6 4   ◇ K Q 8   ♣ 9 2

Overcall 2♡. You are in the 11-13 range but have a nice six-card suit. Also, with a LTC (Losing Trick Count) of six, this hand has good offensive potential.

♠ J 4   ♡ A K 9   ◇ 8 6 5   ♣ A 10 8 4 3

Not this time. At the table, the player with this hand overcalled 2♣ and eventually went -500 while the opponents could only make a partscore. The difference between this hand and the previous one is that it's too balanced, has a LTC of eight and the long suit is nowhere near as good.

♠ 6 2   ♡ A K J 9 6   ◇ 8 5   ♣ A J 8 7

This collection has just enough pluses to persuade me to compete with a 2♡ overcall. The LTC here is seven (two spades, a heart, two diamonds and two clubs), the distribution is mildly unbalanced and you have a good five-card suit.

♠ K Q   ♡ A 10 7 2   ◇ K 9 5 3 2   ♣ J 8

This hand is too flawed for a takeout double of 1♠ because of the doubleton club. How about a 2◇ overcall, then? Again it's a seven-loser hand in the mildly unbalanced category, but there are two crucial differences from the previous hand: almost half the points are in the two doubletons, and the diamonds aren't that robust. That should be enough to deter you from making the two-level overcall.

1NT OVERCALLS

There isn't much difference between opening and overcalling 1NT. However, for safety reasons, you should have a high card in their suit for a 1NT overcall.

The range for a 1NT overcall is just a shade higher at 15-18 and a balanced hand. Vulnerable, you might want to have a source of tricks if you're on the low end of the point count, so as to ward off a disastrous result. Compare these two hands when your RHO opens 1♡:

♠K5 ♡AJ9 ◇KJ1042 ♣A76

♠K86 ♡A54 ◇KQ76 ♣A92

Both hands qualify for a 1NT overcall, but you'd do so confidently on the first example and with a bit more trepidation on the second. If your side is vulnerable, some players might decide on a slightly-flawed takeout double as the less risky option on the 4333 shape, but that's a matter of preference.

HOW ADVANCER PROCEEDS AFTER AN OVERCALL

An opening bid in a suit could be as much as 21 HCP, so you need to respond on as few as 6. Since an overcall is seldom more than 16 or 17 HCP, you do not have to take action on most 6-7 point hands. With 8 or 9 points, you can either raise if you have support or show a good six-card or longer suit at the one-level. Otherwise, hands in this range should pass as there won't be much chance of game.

With 10 or more points, you should be prepared to take a bid. Since the cheapest raise is normally 8-10 points, we have to find a way of describing better hands with support for overcaller's suit. There's sometimes a problem finding a bid, as we can see by contemplating this auction:

LHO	Partner	RHO	You
1♡	2♣	pass	?

♠A1075 ♡95 ◇A863 ♣KJ4

With 12 HCP, your hand is too strong for a simple raise to 3♣ as you have enough points to open the bidding. For those of you curious about what a jump raise of an overcall means, that will be discussed in Chapter 7. For now, let's just note that a jump to 4♣ would bypass 3NT as a potential contract, and that could well be the only game that makes with your balanced hand. Then again, you can't bid notrump yourself with your two small cards in LHO's suit.

Most players nowadays would bid 2♡ with this hand, cuebidding the opponent's suit. What does this mean? Pointwise, 11 or more, with no upper limit. In addition, you should have a fit (three or more cards) or a partial fit (at least Kx) for partner. You probably don't have a stopper in their suit as you haven't bid 2NT or 3NT.

Once you cuebid, you're well-placed whatever overcaller does. If he continues with 2♠, you should then raise him to game. If he has sound values and a heart stopper, you'll hear 2NT and can give him a boost to 3NT. Should he bid the other minor, diamonds, he'll have a better than minimum hand as your cuebid by definition offers 3♣ as a resting spot. So you'd once again forge on to game. If overcaller retreats to 3♣, that suggests a minimum hand, so you'll pass: you lack the points for 5♣ and the heart stopper(s) for 3NT.

Before we leave the topic of overcalls (at least for now), let's consider the meaning of a new suit bid by advancer. A new suit should be a one-round force. That's entirely consistent with the principle of a new suit response to an opening bid being forcing.

LHO	Partner	RHO	You
1♠	2♣	pass	?

If you happen to be in possession of these cards:

♠ J 9 8   ♡ A K 7   ◇ K Q 9 6 3 2   ♣ 8

you'd very much like a 2◇ bid to be forcing, for at least one round. With luck partner will raise or bid notrump, and if he repeats the clubs, you can then decide whether to pass or correct to 3◇.

Ah, but suppose you have:

♠ K 6 2   ♡ J 10 4   ◇ K J 9 8 6 3   ♣ 4

Here you want to mention the diamond suit to 'improve the contract', but can't proceed in that vein as the bid would be forcing. So you're stuck with passing, which isn't necessarily a bad thing, on account of:

• The hand has no game interest to speak of.

- Who's to say that your diamonds are better than his clubs? After all, partner did make a two-level overcall and could easily have a better six-card suit than you do.
- Finally, the opponents might have to bail us out against their will. Since they play negative doubles, opener is expected to reopen with a double if he is short in clubs, as we'll see later. So you might get a belated escape hatch through which to wriggle out into 2◊ later on.

Two Bids or One?

What do these three auctions have in common?

1)

LHO	Partner	RHO	You
1◊	dbl	pass	1♡
pass	1NT		

2)

LHO	Partner	RHO	You
1♠	dbl	pass	2♣
pass	2◊		

3)

LHO	Partner	RHO	You
1◊	1♡	2◊	pass
pass	dbl		

In each of these sequences, partner is showing extra values above and beyond his original call. Moreover, each of these auctions are frequently misinterpreted.

We'll begin with the first two examples, where partner doubles and then bids on. What gives? Does partner have a bare opener and is not enthralled with your suit, clutching hands like:

♠ A 9 6 5	♠ K Q
♡ K 10	♡ A 10 7 2
◊ A Q 3	◊ K 9 5 3 2
♣ J 9 5 4	♣ J 8
for Auction #1	for Auction #2

No, because neither of these hands, even with opening values, should have doubled in the first place, as they were not prepared for the suit you've chosen. Partner would have been best off staying out of the auction for the time being as it is too risky to take immediate action with a minimum balanced hand unless it contains support for all unbid suits.

In the first sequence, the reason partner is removing your 1♡ to notrump is because he has something like:

♠AJ86 ♡KQ5 ◇AJ10 ♣KJ5

This is a hand too good for a direct 1NT overcall, and the only way it can be shown is to double first and then continue with 1NT — showing 19-21 points and a balanced hand. As advancer, therefore, you should be placing the contract in game with 7 or more HCP, and inviting with 5 or 6.

Now look at the second of our auctions. What to make of the 2◇ bid? Again, partner is showing an unusually good hand, along the lines of:

♠K6 ♡AJ8 ◇AK9875 ♣K3

If you're in the habit of looking at the opponents' convention card, you'll see that in most cases their simple overcalls top out at 16 or 17 HCP. Consequently, this hand can only be shown by doubling first and then bidding diamonds.

Finally, in the last of the three auctions, what is overcaller showing? Is it penalty, with him having diamonds as a second suit? One of the principles of competitive bidding is that a double of a partscore is for takeout if the other player hasn't bid, and that is the case here. It doesn't matter that the double was preceded by an overcall. A hand such as:

♠K104 ♡AKJ76 ◇8 ♣KJ92

is not ideal for an immediate takeout double of 1◇ as you have only three spades and the point count falls within the 12-15 HCP range. So you overcalled your nice five-card heart suit. Now that the opponents have bid 2◇, it seems right to compete further with extra values and shortness in their suit, but with what? Instead of rehashing old news, you'd like to give partner new information. So bidding 2♡ now is not the way to go. Neither is 3♣, which increases the level and misses out on a possible spade fit. Double is the most flexible action, and partner should expect approximately this distribution — three spades along with five hearts and three or four clubs.

All of this leads to the idea of contemplating whether you have a good enough hand for a second action before making a decision on what your first one should be. We'll take this auction as an example, and then look at some hands:

LHO	Partner	RHO	You
	pass	1◇	?

♠ A K J 8 3   ♡ J 7 4 2   ◇ 5   ♣ Q 10 6

This is a one-action hand, and with spades so much better than your other suits, I would choose to overcall 1♠ rather than double. With only 11 HCP, you are not worth a second bid even though you have support for hearts and clubs.

♠ A J 5   ♡ K 9 7   ◇ A Q   ♣ K Q 10 6 2

This hand is worth two bids and you should start with a double. You'll follow up with 1NT if partner bids 1♡ or 1♠.

♠ A Q 9 5   ♡ A K 7 4   ◇ 3   ♣ K Q 10 7

A two-action hand again. Double and, if partner bids 1♡ or 1♠, jump raise to three (not game, as partner could have zippo). If LHO raises to 2◇ and it's passed back around to you, double again. Once a takeout double, *always* a takeout double unless they are at the game level.

♠ A Q 8 7   ♡ J 9 6 4 2   ◇ 6   ♣ K Q 9

A one-action hand with only 12 HCP. What should your choice be? You have a five-card suit, true, but it's rather shabby. Moreover, with partner being a passed hand, there's only a faint chance of game, and your primary intent should be to find the best partscore. With nice support for both spades and clubs, the most flexible choice is to bypass the hearts and enter the auction via a takeout double.

The Dos and Don'ts of Negative Doubles

Negative doubles were introduced well over fifty years ago as an alternative treatment to the penalty double of an enemy overcall. They gained popularity almost immediately, and have now achieved universal acceptance among the bridge community. Entire books have been written on them. What I propose to do here is to give a brief introduction to negative doubles and also present a few tips on how to use them properly and to best effect.

A negative double is a first cousin of the takeout double. Let's put the negative double and takeout double side-by-side and note the similarities and differences between the two:

LHO	Partner	RHO	You
		1◇	dbl

LHO	Partner	RHO	You
	1◇	1♡	dbl

In the first auction your double is a takeout double: it is the first action by your side. You'll have support for all three unbid suits and/or a hand of 17 or more HCP.

In the second sequence your double is a negative double and is the second action by your side, preceded by an opening bid from partner and an overcall on your right. The negative double shows at least 6 points and is a takeout for the remaining two suits, spades and clubs. The usual range for a negative double is between 6 and 12 points, although it could be more if responder is balanced without a five-card suit.

With this in mind, we can now explore some guidelines for negative doubles.

1) Be cognizant of the level.

The level of the interference will dictate the number of points you should have if you are thinking about making a negative double. Let's look at three hands that all include both major suits:

a) ♠K 10 6 5 ♡Q J 7 3 ◇8 6 3 ♣J 6
b) ♠Q 8 7 2 ♡A J 9 5 ◇9 8 4 ♣Q 10
c) ♠A J 5 2 ♡K J 8 6 ◇10 7 ♣Q 6 3

Partner opens 1♣ and RHO is about to overcall in diamonds. If he bids 1◇, you can make a negative double with all three hands, even the 7-count of hand (a), because for the time being you can play a major suit at the one-level.

If righty makes a jump overcall of 2◇, you can still make the negative double with (b) and (c), but should pass with hand (a). You will have to play at the two-level for sure (maybe even the three-level if opener has to bid his clubs again), and to do that, you need at least 8-9 points to be on reasonably safe ground.

In a third case, where the nasty person on your right preempts all the way to 3◇, you now are committed to the three-level with any action you take, so you need 10 or more points to compete. Accordingly, you should pass with both (a) and (b), and only venture in with a negative double on hand (c).

2) *You must have two places to play to make a negative double.*

If your hand cannot support two of the three suits not mentioned by the overcaller, then you should not make a negative double. We'll use a slightly different auction as our reference point:

LHO	Partner	RHO	You
	1◇	1♡	?

And your sprinkling of trinkets can be:

♠ A J 8 4   ♡ Q 5 4 3   ◇ 8 6   ♣ K 9 8

This hand cannot make a negative double as it only contains spades. With 10 HCP, you're worth a bid, but the action you take should be a bid of 1♠. A new suit by responder, even in a competitive auction, might only be a four-card suit if bid at the one-level. However, a new suit at the *two-level* in competition should be five or more.

♠ Q 8 5 4   ♡ 10 3   ◇ K 6   ♣ K 9 8 5 3

A classic negative double. You have both unbid suits, spades and clubs, and will be quite happy if opener bids either of them. If partner bids 1NT or 2◇ instead, you will pass

♠ A 9 5 2   ♡ 6 5   ◇ A J 8 4   ♣ 10 9 7

I would make a negative double with this hand as well. Wait a minute, didn't I say we needed *both* of the unbid suits to make a negative double? What if opener goes nuts in the club suit? That won't be such a catastrophe, as you simply go back to diamonds, and partner will be satisfied with your two aces and four-card support. This meets the 'two ports in a storm' criterion for a negative double — you can't support both unbid suits, but you can support one of them, along with partner's first-bid suit.

3) *With opening values, bid a five-card suit instead of making a negative double.*

Suppose you have in your possession this delightful assortment:

♠ K J 5 3   ♡ 4   ◇ K 6   ♣ A Q J 5 3 2

Partner opens 1◇ and your right-hand opponent bids 1♡. You *do* have both unbid suits here, spades and clubs. Despite this, you should not make a negative double.

Why not? It's more important to give partner a very clear idea of how strong your hand is. If you make a negative double, you could have as few as 6 HCP. If partner doesn't cooperate by bidding spades, he might not treat a later club bid by you as forcing. If you bid 2♣ immediately, opener will play you for 11 or more HCP as you've introduced a new suit at the two-level as responder. You can always get the spade suit in later regardless of how the bidding progresses. Even if the opponents bid all the way up to 4♡, you can now bring the spades into focus by competing to 4♠. Then partner can choose between the black-suit games, knowing that you have at least opening values.

4) Opener has to be aware of his responsibilities.

Opener has an important role to play in the negative double scheme of things. One of his responsibilities is to make an appropriate rebid when partner makes a negative double. The other is to keep the bidding alive if the overcall is passed around to him and he has shortness in LHO's suit.

First, we'll examine what to rebid as opener when partner makes a negative double. With 12 to a bad 15 you should take some minimum action. With a good 15 to 17, make a stronger bid, and with 18 or more, drive to a game. Let's look at some examples:

Partner	RHO	You	LHO
		1◇	1♡
dbl	pass	?	

♠K86 ♡A94 ◇KJ103 ♣Q75

Rebid 1NT with your balanced hand.

♠A8 ♡765 ◇AJ104 ♣KJ98

No heart stopper, so 1NT is out of the question. Bid 2♣ as partner will have spades and one of the minors, usually clubs, for the negative double.

♠AQ105 ♡96 ◇KQJ54 ♣K7

The loser count (five) and a good 15 HCP argue for a jump to 2♠, which should indicate a hand that's at least a king better than a minimum opening bid.

♠K4 ♡73 ◇AKJ1083 ♣KQ2

You're blessed with a good hand and a strong suit. Jump to 3◇, just as you would have if LHO had stayed quiet and partner had made a one-level response.

♠A74 ♡1042 ◇KJ965 ♣AQ

Nothing appeals as a rebid choice here. Probably the least of evils is to rebid 2◇ — at least you have five of them.

Now let's discuss the other aspect of opener's responsibilities, with this sequence rolling back around to you:

Partner	RHO	You	LHO
		1♡	1♠
pass	pass	?	

We need to take stock of the bidding to this point and draw the necessary conclusions. What can partner *not* have? He isn't likely to have support for hearts, as he didn't raise. He doesn't have responding values with the minor suits, it would appear, as he's failed to make a negative double. Nor will he be in the 8-10 range with a spade stopper, as he would have bid 1NT with that hand. That means partner can only have one of two hands:

a) a hand with some points and lots of spades that would have liked to made a penalty double of 1♠ but couldn't because you are playing negative doubles.

b) a mediocre to putrid hand, lacking support for your original suit.

If you have a nice hand of 16+ points, partner could have either of these two hands. If you're in the lower range of 12-15, he is far more likely to have hand (a), or the 'trap pass', as we refer to it. Why does he rate to have the better hand? It's mostly because your RHO did not act. With any smattering of values or trump support, advancer would have made some kind of noise. So if he has a baddish hand *without* trump support, what do you think partner has?

This now leads us into what opener should do when the overcall gets passed back around to him. If you're short in overcaller's suit, you should be getting back in. If partner has the type (a) hand, you may have a sizeable penalty to collect from defending their contract, and if he has type (b), you should be able to scramble out to a playable trump fit at the two-level.

So now, let's look at possible hands for opener to judge whether or not to reenter the battleground on the auction above:

♠ Q 7 4   ♡ A K 10 9 3   ◇ A 10 5   ♣ 5 4

Don't even think about bidding. Your Qxx of spades suggests that partner does not have the trap pass and is far more apt to be in possession of the type (b) hand.

♣ 6   ♡ A J 10 6 5   ◇ J x   ♣ K Q J 9 4

Partner may well have hand (a) and be chomping at the bit for you to reopen with a double, but alas, this is not the hand where you can oblige him. With a two-suiter and less on defense than you'd expect from an opening hand, you should bid 2♣ here and let partner choose between hearts and clubs.

♠ 9   ♡ K Q 10 8 7 2   ◇ K Q J   ♣ J 6 3

Bidding 2♡ is the only sensible option here. Note that in the realm of negative doubles, opener is always going to act with shortness in the enemy suit. When he bids instead of doubling in passout chair, that indicates an unbalanced hand that is not very promising for defending a low-level contract by the opponents.

♠ 7   ♡ A K 9 6 4   ◇ A Q 8   ♣ J 9 5 2

Finally, we get to the hand where you can reopen with a double. It doesn't matter which of the two hand types partner has, you are prepared for either of them. If he has the trap pass, you have more than enough defense to rack up a hefty number against 1♠ doubled. If he has the pile of junk, then he'll bid his longest suit and you will be able to survive whatever two-level contract you land in.

Better Late than Immediately or Never: Delayed Actions

Just because a hand is not suited to entering the bidding right away doesn't mean you have to remain silent forever. There are two breeds of competitive auctions. One is where the double, overcall or preempt takes place right way. However, while some auctions begin as uncontested, often the other side makes a delayed entry or balances when the auction grinds to a halt.

Delayed actions (competing after both opponents have bid) and balancing will be covered in detail in Chapter 5. To whet your appetite, though, I'll revisit an earlier hand.

LHO	Partner	RHO	You
		1♠	pass
1NT	pass	2♣	?

♠ K Q   ♡ A 10 7 2   ◇ K 9 5 3 2   ♣ J 8

As I've explained previously, this hand doesn't have enough club support for a takeout double and the five-card suit is not good enough for an immediate two-level overcall. However, now that opener has bid clubs as well as spades, you are finally in a position to compete sensibly without misdescribing your hand. Since a double here would be the first action for your side and there are still two unbid suits, it would be takeout for diamonds and hearts. Ideally, partner will have length in one of the red suits and you'll either buy the contract at the two-level or force the opponents higher.

Oh, for the Good Old Days of the Penalty Double

One of the recent trends in bridge practice has been a veering away from the penalty double. It all began with the use of a negative double when the opponents overcall. That development was a useful one, and the fact that negative doubles are widely accepted in modern bridge attests to their value. However, it hasn't stopped there; there has been a massive influx of conventional doubles to replace the natural ones. I'll touch on many of them over the course of this book.

At any rate, while I've never been one to get in the way of progress, keeping the 'gotcha!' business double in your quiver is entirely appropriate and sensible in certain auctions. I'll address two of them that are often a source of confusion.

LHO	Partner	RHO	You
		1♡	dbl
1NT	dbl		

What is partner's double of 1NT? It should be for penalty. Why not for takeout? The answer is that both members of the partnership should not be making a takeout double on the same hand. If he wants to compete at the two-level, partner should bid his longest suit since your takeout double has indicated support for all of the unbid suits. Partner should have at least 9 or 10 points, doesn't think they can make 1NT, and has some interest in wielding the axe if they scurry out to the two-level.

LHO	Partner	RHO	You
			1NT
2◇	dbl		

A growing number of players use this as a 'stolen bid' double, meaning that partner is transferring to hearts in this auction. This is a misguided notion, to my way of thinking. Double should be penalty, while 2♡ or 2♠ by responder would be natural signoffs.

Why? Well, let's have a glance at this trio of hands for responder:

a) ♠875 ♡KJ863 ◇92 ♣Q104
b) ♠A106 ♡108 ◇K985 ♣10972
c) ♠974 ♡1062 ◇A108 ♣KJ94

Pairs that use a double of 2◇ as a transfer to hearts may gain slightly on hand (a), although it might make no difference who is the declarer in a heart contract. Conversely, however, the 'stolen bid' double deprives you of a lucrative penalty on hand (b) as you'd have to pass or overbid with 2NT. Hand (c) is also one where you could surely beat them several in 2◇ as you have at least 23 HCP while they have at best an eight-card fit and perhaps not even that.

QUIZ HANDS

1)   ♠872 ♡10 ◇KQ42 ♣Q9632

Your side is vulnerable, and after you pass initially, everyone else has something to say:

West	North	East	South
			pass
1♠	dbl	2♠	?

Is there any reason to bid here? Or should you just hold your tongue? What's your vote?

2)   ♠6 ♡1082 ◇AK86 ♣J8742

Your side is vulnerable, with RHO having stepped in after partner has opened.

West	North	East	South
	1♠	2♡	?

East has made a two-level overcall, and responder now has to decide whether or not to get involved. What is your inclination?

3)   ♠K8 ♡KJ983 ◇K7 ♣A1043

Both sides are vulnerable, and the bidding starts out:

West	North	East	South
1◇	1♠	pass	?

Pretty nice hand when partner makes a vulnerable overcall. What now?

4)   ♠A9765 ♡AJ95 ◇Q932 ♣—

You are vulnerable against not. Partner passes and RHO opens 1♣. Should you compete and if so, in what manner?

1)   North-South vul.

♠ 8 7 2   ♡ 10   ◇ K Q 4 2   ♣ Q 9 6 3 2

West	North	East	South
			pass
1♠	dbl	2♠	?

Bid 3♣. They have a fit in spades, but your side has one in clubs with partner's takeout double guaranteeing at least three of them. Even if North is minimum, the points will be divided fairly evenly between the two sides and it's seldom right to allow them to declare a two-level partscore when there is a likely trump fit your way. The entire deal is:

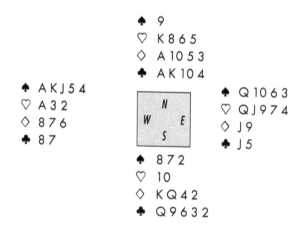

East-West can make eight tricks in spades, so passing with the South hand will yield a poor result. Meanwhile 3♣ makes your way, so the best the opponents can do is compete further to 3♠ for down one, still a better score for you than minus 110.

2)   North-South vul.

♠6 ♡10 8 2 ◇A K 10 6 ♣J 8 7 4 2

West	North	East	South
	1♠	2♡	?

Pass. A negative double that will propel your side to the three-level needs in the vicinity of 10 points, or at least a very good 9-count. There are also two other drawbacks to competing with this hand: there is no fit with opener's spade suit, and besides, the 'death holding' in hearts maximizes the potential losers there. The full layout is:

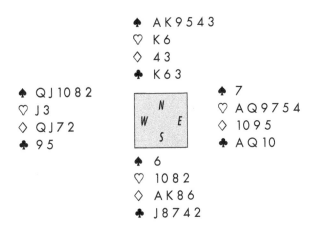

Your side will have no problem defeating their 2♡ contract. Two diamonds and a ruff, then ace and another spade will eventually promote your ♡10. After that, declarer will still have some work to do in the heart and club suits. A negative double on insufficient values will yield the opposite result, as partner will have to repeat the spades and that won't be a pleasant result. If you pass instead, opener will probably *not* reopen as he'll take a dim view of his ♡Kx in front of overcaller.

3)   Both vul.

♠ K 8   ♡ K J 9 8 3   ◇ K 7   ♣ A 10 4 3

West	North	East	South
1◇	1♠	pass	?

If the partnership agreement is that a new suit is forcing here, you can bring your long suit into the picture right away with 2♡, as the overcaller cannot pass.

Partner will raise hearts and you can now press on to game, with a happy result:

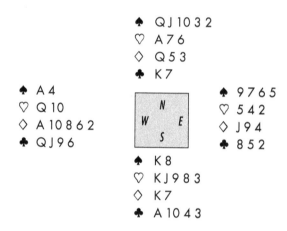

```
              ♠ Q J 10 3 2
              ♡ A 7 6
              ◇ Q 5 3
              ♣ K 7
♠ A 4                           ♠ 9 7 6 5
♡ Q 10          N               ♡ 5 4 2
◇ A 10 8 6 2  W   E             ◇ J 9 4
♣ Q J 9 6         S             ♣ 8 5 2
              ♠ K 8
              ♡ K J 9 8 3
              ◇ K 7
              ♣ A 10 4 3
```

Dummy's spades will establish for pitches, so 4♡ will make even if declarer loses a trump because there are only two immediate losers.

Partnerships that play a new suit bid as non-forcing after an overcall would have much more trouble describing this hand.

4) North-South vul.

♠A9765 ♡AJ95 ♢Q932 ♣—

West	North	East	South
	pass	1♣	?

Yes, the hand does contain a five-card suit. However, before sailing in with a 1♠ overcall, consider whether this is a one- or two-bid hand. With only 11 HCP, you can't really take any further action if you bid 1♠ initially. Since it's only worth one action, the best course is to make a takeout double, as you have good support for all three unbid suits. Having doubled, though, you absolutely cannot bid the spades later as that would promise a much better hand. Once you've made your one peep, it's up to partner to set the contract for your side. The whole hand is:

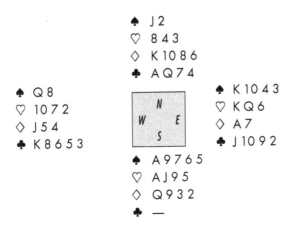

```
              ♠ J 2
              ♡ 8 4 3
              ◇ K 10 8 6
              ♣ A Q 7 4
  ♠ Q 8                      ♠ K 10 4 3
  ♡ 10 7 2         N         ♡ K Q 6
  ◇ J 5 4       W     E      ◇ A 7
  ♣ K 8 6 5 3      S         ♣ J 10 9 2
              ♠ A 9 7 6 5
              ♡ A J 9 5
              ◇ Q 9 3 2
              ♣ —
```

West will raise to 2♣ over the double, and North should compete with 2◇. This will become the final contract, unless responder decides to repeat his story and bid 3♣, in which case North will double and East-West will go down at least three for a horrid result.

CHAPTER 2

HOW HIGH CAN YOU FLY?

The first chapter of this book dealt primarily with the three main linchpins of competitive bidding, namely the takeout double, the simple overcall and the negative double. These actions are usually constructive in nature, and can have a variety of results, sometimes arriving at game, but more often waging a partscore battle.

These next two chapters will complete the toolbox of immediate actions, before the focus shifts towards later stages in the auction. The remaining arrows in the quiver are preempts (including weak two-bids) and two-suited overcalls. The big change is that these salvos will typically force the opponents (and your side as well) to the three-level or beyond to vie for the contract. They tend to be more obstructive in their intent, depriving both you and the opponents of convenient bidding room. While the higher-level actions don't necessarily require a lot of high-card values, it's imperative that the bidder has an unbalanced hand to provide a measure of security in such dangerous waters.

Preemptive bidding

Preemptive opening bids by their nature impart a certain degree of chaos to any auction. Preempts appeal to the kid in us, and some women might say they hold a certain attraction for the perpetually disorganized male species as well. It's our way of saying to the opponents, 'No, you are *not* going to have a nice, tidy, efficient bidding sequence to arrive at your best spot. We are going to mess things up right off the bat and you'll just have to cope with it.' That's why, even though they are opening bids, preempts have their place in a book on competitive bidding — when we use them, there is an assumption that the hand probably belongs to the opponents, and we're getting our obstruction in before they can even start bidding.

Most people are familiar with the general characteristics of a preemptive opening. It's a seven-card or longer suit in the case of a three-level or higher opening bid, and precisely a six-card suit if it's a weak two-bid. First- and second-seat preempts are limited to a maximum of 10 high card points. They also tend to deny a running suit headed by the AKQ. With either 11 or more HCP or a solid seven-card or longer suit, you should be opening at the one-level. Third- and fourth-seat preempts are a different breed and will be covered in the wrap-up of weak two-bids later on.

Within the realm of preempting, however, there are many different styles and philosophies. Some players like to have tightly-defined parameters, while others tend to be less stringent. The former group likes to have a good picture of the trick-taking potential for both sides. The latter group is willing to sacrifice accuracy in order to be able to preempt more frequently.

You might assume from this that you can either be sensibly aggressive in your preempts or decide instead to be wild and woolly. However, there are, in fact, not two but three styles of preempting.

Sound preemptors: These players employ the Rule of 2 and 3 when preempting. That means being within two tricks of your bid if you are vulnerable, and within three if you are not vulnerable.

Light preemptors: This sub-group is not quite so demanding in number of tricks required. Some of them will use the Rule of 2, 3 and 4 (within two tricks at unfavorable colors, three tricks at equal vulnerability, four tricks if they're not vulnerable against vulnerable). Others won't use any rule at all, and just get in there with any half-decent suit. To illustrate the difference in styles, consider this hand:

♠5 ♡KJ98643 ◇Q76 ♣82

Sound preemptors will only open 3♡ if they are not vulnerable, and pass otherwise. Light preemptors will sneer that 'vulnerability is for accountants' and open 3♡ regardless of the colors.

Undisciplined: Sound and light preemptors are agreed on one thing, that you should have little if any defense outside of your long suit. A preempt is considered to be 'undisciplined' if the hand has defensive tricks outside the long suit, or if it contains a side four-card major.

Here are three hands to illustrate the difference between the three schools of preempting:

♠4 ♡KQ108653 ◇Q105 ♣96

This collection would be universally opened with 3♡.

♠ K 8   ♡ 7   ◊ Q J 9 8 6 5 4   ♣ J 10 9

The 'sound' community would not open this hand with 3◊. The light preemptors might, and the undisciplined school definitely would.

♠ A 3   ♡ J 9 8 7 6 5 2   ◊ K 8 5   ♣ 9

An undisciplined soul might well decide to open 3♡ with this hand. With two possible outside defensive tricks, neither the sound nor the light preemptors would consider that option.

You may have heard the expression 'furthering the preempt'. Suppose partner opens 3◊ and your RHO makes a takeout double. You are not vulnerable against vulnerable opponents and have:

♠ 8 6   ♡ A 9 5   ◊ Q 7 2   ♣ K Q 9 6 5

You should bid 5◊ in normal circumstances. Since a standard preempt (sound or light) has virtually nothing on the outside, your expectation is that they can make 4♡ or 4♠, and even if your sacrifice goes down two or three, you'll still be in a gain position.

However, if your partner may have values outside the long suit, taking sacrifices and furthering the preempt go out the window. Now you may go down two or three in 5◊ against a game that was destined to fail their way. It's difficult to judge the trick-taking ability for each side when your partnership is inclined to undisciplined preempts. You will often have to let the initial bid serve as the roadblock for the opponents, as the total picture for your side is no longer written in stone.

RESPONDING TO A THREE-LEVEL PREEMPT

Let's say partner opens a non-vulnerable 3♡ and you have this nice assortment of goodies:

♠ K J 6 4   ♡ 5   ◊ K 9 8 7   ♣ A K J 2

It may break your heart to do it, but the likely winning action is to hold your tongue and pass. The person holding this 15-count bid 3NT, forgetting that a preempt should deny a running suit. Partner laid down:

♠ 3   ♡ K Q 10 7 6 4 2   ◊ 6 4 3   ♣ 7 5

which is definitely in the ballpark as far as preempts go. If the defense leads spades against 3NT, you'll be lucky to get five or six tricks. The same problem exists in 4♡, where you could lose three diamonds (or two diamonds and a ruff), with the major suit aces to come for down two.

This illustrates two things you should keep in mind when partner preempts. One is that 3NT isn't going to make unless you have enough for partner's suit to run or a good long suit of your own. The second is that points aren't especially relevant, but *tricks* are. Let's pair up the hand just above with a new hand we've dealt you:

♠A 8 6 5   ♡J   ◇A K J 8   ♣Q 10 8 6

♠3   ♡K Q 10 7 6 4 2   ◇6 4 3   ♣7 5

Another 15-point hand, but this one gives 4♡ a reasonable play. The difference between this hand and the other one is that you have a filler in partner's long suit and 'hard' values (aces and kings). Those are always good to have when partner is showing a long suit with not much outside. Note, however, that 3NT will again have no play on a black-suit lead. Usually, the preemptor is going to wind up declaring the hand in his or her suit. The major question is at what level.

What about a new suit response to a preempt? Should it be forcing or not? When partner is showing a seven-card or longer suit for a three-level opening, it doesn't seem logical to try and fight him for the right to name the trump suit, as that would just be asking for trouble. As a result, I'd play a new suit as forcing for one round. However, we'll come back to the new-suit issue in the upcoming discussion on weak two-bids, since in that case opener is promising fewer cards in his long suit.

DEFENDING AGAINST A PREEMPTIVE OPENING

When the opponents preempt at the three-level or higher and you are thinking of competing, this is the recommended framework:

Double   Takeout at the three-level, and you should probably use it as takeout if they open a natural 4♣ or 4◇ as well.

   If they open 4♡, most partnerships use double as enough tricks to beat it, but promise spade tolerance (three or more) in case advancer wants to bail out to a five-card or longer spade suit.

   Doubles of opening bids of 4♠ or higher are suggestive of penalties — not a trump stack (which you'll almost never have), but plenty of high cards. The reason is that you won't often want to be playing at the five-level. If you want to do something other than double, the options are to bid a six-card or longer suit if you have one, or bid 4NT, which in this case is *not* an ace-asking bid, but a general takeout with support for two or three suits (and mucho high-card points)

3NT   This has a fairly wide range because of their preempt. It could be as few as a good 16 HCP, or as many as 21 or 22. Hands in the lower echelon should either have a source of tricks or a holding in their suit where you can duck one or two rounds (such as Ax or Axx).

Bids   Direct-seat actions should be very sound, justified by either 15+ HCP or nice distributional features. If the opponents open 3◇, either of these hands would merit a 3♠ overcall:

♠ A K 10 8 2   ♡ A J 7   ◇ 9 4   ♣ K Q 10
♠ A Q 9 7 6 4   ♡ A 10 8   ◇ 3   ♣ Q J 7

The first hand has 17 HCP, the second hand is minimum in points but contains a six-card suit and shortness in diamonds.

When they've opened at the three-level, you should assume a useful 7 points in partner's hand and determine whether your hand is good enough to play opposite that for the level you might be contracting at. Sometimes LHO will have all the stuff and partner has the dregs, or on the brighter side, partner could have opening or near-opening values. So the 'rule of 7' is a compromise between the best- and worst-case scenarios.

Most 12-14 point balanced hands should pass when the opponents start off with a preempt. For example, with them firing the 3◇ salvo on your right, if you have:

♠ A Q 7 6 4   ♡ K 8 5   ◇ 4 2   ♣ K J 7

you should pass. You'll need a lot from partner to make 3♠ — a fit and the ability to cover three of your losers. Bidding 3♠ now can't really succeed as partner will carry on to game if he has that magic hand, and if he has anything less, your LHO will be expressing the opinion via the red card that you're in a world of trouble. A definite warning sign on this hand is that your values are not sure tricks. If partner doesn't have the aces to match up with your kings, they'll be sitting on your left as the preemptor won't have much to speak of outside his long suit.

A USEFUL RECIPE FOR SPADE PREEMPTS

Suppose you pick up a hand like this:

♠ K 10　♡ A K 9 5　◇ Q 3　♣ A Q 9 5 2

and your RHO opens 3♠, with neither side vulnerable. How do you feel about the situation? Not particularly good, I suspect, as you have three options available to you, each of them flawed. With 18 HCP, you have to do *something*, as it's unlikely that partner will be able to scrounge up any kind of balancing action. Let's examine the alternatives.

Bidding 3NT is right on points but since you won't be able to hold up on the first round of spades if they are led, you'll be going down unless you have nine tricks off the top. Overcalling 4♣ bypasses 3NT and could also miss out on a heart fit. A takeout double keeps hearts in the picture, but what if partner bids diamonds?

Now let's say the same RHO opens 4♠ instead of 3♠. Does your hand justify taking the bidding to the five-level? No, it doesn't. Wading in with 5332 or 5422 shape is not going to result in a happy ending the majority of the time. You need a six-card suit, or 5-5 or 6-5 distribution — something along those lines. So what is the only feasible choice that your RHO has left you? That would be to double and take whatever money you're entitled to.

Dave Brough, who I've played with as a partner and teammate, once made the curious observation that '3♠ is more preemptive than 4♠'. It took me a while to grasp what he was driving at, but eventually the light clicked on. 3♠ is, in fact, the most deadly and effective of all the preempts. It gives the opponents 3NT and the four-level in a suit, but those could all be very risky propositions for them. If they bid, partner can now either double them or, if they've managed to land on their feet, continue on to 4♠ if it looks right for our side.

After a 4♠ opening, on the other hand, the luster goes off most of the *bids* for the opponents. What they are left with is the shrug-your-shoulders-and-double choice. When you open 4♠, you'll often be left to play that contract. The only question is whether or not you are going to be doubled. The reason is that you've severely limited the range of viable (and possibly losing) options for them, the antithesis of what an effective preempt should do.

A 4♠ opening, therefore, should promise a suit of eight-plus cards *or* a hand that will be able to make game opposite a few useful cards from partner. Here are a couple of hands to illustrate:

♠ A Q J 9 8 7 5　♡ 4　◇ Q J 10 7　♣ 6

♠ A Q J 10 6 4 3　♡ 10 7　◇ 8　♣ Q 10 5

Some might be tempted to open 4♠ at favorable vulnerability with each of these hands. It's a reasonable thought on the first hand, as it has two ways to succeed. With a loser count of five, if partner has a little something in spades and/or diamonds, your contract will have a play. Moreover, they could be making 4♡ their way. The latter hand has too many flaws to go that high. You have one extra loser, two possible tricks on defense, and your doubleton heart reduces the likelihood of the opponents having a fit there. The opponents may not even have game their way so any minus, doubled or not, rates to be bad for your side. On the second hand, opening 3♠ is enough, letting partner choose the final destination.

MINOR-SUIT PREEMPTS AT THE FOUR- AND FIVE-LEVEL

A 4♣ or 4♢ opening should typically be a broken eight-card suit, lacking two of the top three honors. In addition, the hand should have no interest whatsoever in a 3NT contract. Usually, the four-level preemptor will be extremely short in one or both majors. I picked up such a hand a few months ago:

♠6   ♡9   ♢KJ987543   ♣Q95

and duly opened 4♢. As you can see, this bid conveys the message of a long minor with no particular interest in a 3NT contract. Note that there are far too many losers for opening 5♢ to be a profitable action.

Opening 5♣ and 5♢ preempts have just as freakish distribution, but unlike their four-level counterparts, there should be some expectation of a make if partner has one or two key values. As with the 4♣ opening, the opponents' default action on the majority of these sequences will be to double, as not many hands will come along where they are secure taking a bid at the five-level. Keeping that in mind, a suitable candidate for the immediate launch to game in a minor would be:

♠—   ♡K74   ♢6   ♣AQ10986542

WEAK TWO-BIDS AND RESPONSES

The weak two-bid is quite simply a variant of a preemptive opening, the main difference being that it normally shows a six-card suit rather than seven or more of them. The range is the same, 5-10 HCP. Some pairs make it 5-9, as their style would be to open at the one-level with most 10-counts. That is a matter of choice.

There's more of a 'safety margin' for playing weak two-bids in an undisciplined manner than for three-level preempts. With a three-level opening, partner has to make an immediate decision. Game or partscore?

My suit or his? Notrump or a suit contract? The information he has to go on is far murkier if the partnership is fond of undisciplined preempts, and there is no operating room for him to seek a clarification of your hand.

If the auction begins with a weak two-bid, we have a tool to inquire for additional information, that being the artificial 2NT response. There are two main variations of it to choose from. They are:

- The 'Feature Ask'
- Ogust responses

The Feature Ask works best with practitioners of the sound weak two-bid, where opener has KJ109xx at the very worst. In that style, responder has no real concerns about the long suit, and just wants to know if opener has any outside values.

Ogust is intended more for those who'd venture a weak two-bid with any six-card suit, regardless of quality, and anything from 5 to a bad 10 HCP. The Ogust responses to 2NT enable responder to learn about both the point range and the quality of opener's suit.

That's the short version. Now we'll flesh out the details:

Feature Ask

Opener	Responder
2♡	2NT
?	

Opener now describes his hand with:

3♣/3♢/3♠   High card in the bid suit, usually ace or king. If it's only the queen, it should have at least two cards with it and opener will be at the top of his range.

3♡   No outside value other than maybe an unguarded queen. Opener will have his good suit and not much else.

3NT   No outside value but the best possible holding in the long suit, at least AKQxxx.

Ogust

Opener	Responder
2♡	2NT
?	

For the purposes of the descriptions below, 'good hand' would mean 8+ HCP and 'good suit' would be two of the top three honors, or something close, like AJ109. Opener will describe his hand by rebidding as follows:

3♣	bad hand, bad suit.
3◇	bad hand, good suit.
3♡	good hand, bad suit.
3♠	good hand, good suit.

One topic you should address with partner is the meaning of a new suit by responder after a weak two-bid. With some pairs, it is a forcing action, but for others it is merely suggestive of a better place to play. Since it's a matter of choice, I'll limit myself to a brief reference to it in the next paragraph.

To sum up, the best structure for responding to a weak two-bid is:

- Regardless of which style two-bids you are playing, the single raise is non-forcing and mildly obstructive in nature.
- Playing 'classical' weak two-bids, all other bids are forward-going. A response of 2NT asks for a feature and new suits are forcing for one round.
- Playing undisciplined weak two-bids, 2NT is Ogust. As for new suits by responder, it's a partnership decision. You can either:
  » Retain them as forcing bids, or...
  » Use them as 'contract improvement', promising a good long suit of your own but no fit or game interest. If you adopt the latter treatment, the 2NT response will then be the only forcing bid and must be the first response on all game-going hands.

One last thing. If a new suit by responder is forcing in your structure, how should the weak-two bidder continue the auction? With a doubleton honor or better in partner's suit, he should raise. With no support but an outside high card, he can bid that suit. With a misfit and nothing extra, he just goes back to his original suit.

THIRD- AND FOURTH-SEAT PREEMPTS

Even sound preemptors will agree that being in third seat after two passes gives you a bit more license to stir the pot. For one thing, you don't have to worry about partner taking you seriously and vaulting your side too high since he's known to have less than an opening bid. The only time he'll bid to game is as a sacrifice against the enemy contract. There's also more to gain since your LHO must have at least an opening bid and possibly a very strong hand. So in third seat you might routinely see non-vulnerable preempts on hands like these:

♠x ♡K 10 8 x x x x ◇x x ♣J x x

♠x ♡x x ◇Q 10 x x ♣K Q 9 x x x

On the flip side, some players might 'preempt' in third seat with full opening bids, such as:

♠x x ♡x x ◇Q J x ♣A K Q 10 x x

'Why?' you might ask. With relative shortness in both majors, they don't expect their side to buy the contract at the one- or two-level. Ergo, they simply bid right away to where they figure they'll have to go eventually.

What we're seeing here, then, is that in third seat, preempts can be more undisciplined, and can be made on anything from total garbage all the way to an opening bid with a long suit. You are purposely generating a murky situation, and that's fine since you know the guy in fourth chair with his opening hand must take his first stab in bidding at the three-level.

In fourth chair, however, you shouldn't be opening with a traditional weak preempt since the opponents are already out of the auction and you could merely pass out the hand for a likely good result. The so-called 'preemptive' bids in passout chair *do* guarantee a long suit of quality. They also suggest 11-14 HCP, something like:

♠A Q J 10 x x ♡x ◇K J x ♣J x x

for a 'weak' two-bid, and

♠x ♡A x ◇x x x ♣A K J 9 x x x

for a three-level preempt. You're opening at a higher level to preclude the opponents from locating a fit (hearts on the first hand, spades on the second) and also suggesting a long suit with opening points in case partner has the top end of a passed hand and is able to try for game.

Jump Overcalls

In a competitive auction where the opponents have opened the bidding, introducing your suit one level higher than you need to doesn't show an especially strong hand pointwise. Why is that? We've already seen in Chapter 1 that with a very good hand you can either make a simple overcall or start with a double and then bid your long suit.

For jump overcalls at the three-level, you can adopt whatever style you and your partner have decided upon for preemptive openings, because aside from their opening bid, the landscape is very much the same.

Two-level jump overcalls are a horse of a different color, however. By definition, they can't be strong, but precisely how weak *are* they? In our initial overcall discussion, some hands in the 8-10 range were deemed to be adequate for one-level action. Therefore, while an opening bid of 2♡ or 2♠ is 5-10 HCP and can sometimes even lead to a game contract, a jump overcall to the two-level in the same suits would be on the low end of a weak two and perhaps even lighter than that. One of my long-standing partners, who is normally is quite sound in his bidding, made it clear to me that this was the one exception, and to his mind it is completely destructive in nature. A quartet of hands will suffice to illustrate, using this auction as our backdrop:

LHO	Partner	RHO	You
		1♣	?

♠K Q 10 8 4 3 ♡6 ◇10 9 7 ♣A 9 5

Despite the modest point-count, this hand is quite respectable with a good suit, shortness and an outside ace. A simple overcall has a bit more appeal than the weak jump to 2♠

♠K J 10 7 3 2 ♡8 6 ◇Q J 4 ♣9 8

Here a jump overcall of 2♠ should be the choice. It describes the suit length, takes away some bidding room from them, and suggests that your hand isn't that good pointwise.

$$\spadesuit K\,10\,8\,7\,6\,4 \quad \heartsuit 2 \quad \diamondsuit J\,9\,7\,6 \quad \clubsuit 8\,3$$

I've seen people bravely leap to 2♠ on this hand if they are not vulnerable, so yes, the weak jump overcall can possibly be that meager. One thing in its favor is that you have unbalanced shape and tolerably decent spots.

$$\spadesuit Q\,9\,6\,5\,4\,3 \quad \heartsuit Q\,4 \quad \diamondsuit J\,8\,7 \quad \clubsuit 6\,5$$

I've also seen them trot out the weak jump overcall on hands of this ilk, which have much less to recommend them. The suit is ragged, besides which you have less distribution and there's not as high a probability that the opponents have a heart fit.

COUNTERING JUMP OVERCALLS — HIGH-LEVEL NEGATIVE DOUBLES

When negative doubles took the stage, they were used in a limited fashion, generally only through 1♠ or 2♠ interference by the opponents. That has all changed and nowadays when we glance at other partnerships' convention cards, we often see them played up to 4◇ or even through the entire four-level. Is this development a good thing? Generally, yes, provided that you keep two things in mind when making the higher-level negative doubles:

1) Remember to add a few points for each level you're being jostled up to in the bidding. Accordingly, if a negative double propels you into four-level territory, support for the other suits *and* near-opening values are a must.
2) In the above situation, if your hand is purely offensive, bid rather than double. If opener doesn't have a standout action, he might elect to pass with a normal balanced hand. To handle that possibility, you should have something tangible to contribute on defense. Suppose the bidding has gone:

LHO	Partner	RHO	You
	1♡	4♣	?

$$\spadesuit K\,J\,9\,4 \quad \heartsuit J\,8 \quad \diamondsuit K\,Q\,J\,9\,7\,6 \quad \clubsuit 5$$

Bid 4◇. A negative double could easily get passed, and you could be either missing a 5◇ game or worse yet, not even beating 4♣ their way. Your bid is forcing, and if partner bids spades or raises, that is good.

A 4♡ rebid by him is not as convenient, but it won't be a tragedy either, with Jx in his suit and a singleton club.

♠ K 10 7 3   ♡ 6 4   ◇ A Q J 8 2   ♣ J 9

A negative double is much better with this hand. You have all the bases covered and should net a decent score regardless of what partner does. With shortness in clubs, partner will bid, and on the off chance that he leaves in your double, you have enough ammo for defense.

Most pairs opt to play negative doubles at least through 3◇, and some use them all the way up to 4♠. Typically, my partners and I select 4◇ as the cutoff point beyond which doubles by responder are more penalty-oriented. Everyone has their own opinion, though, and you can always begin with something and adjust the upper limit for your negative double later based on your in-game experience.

A Wrap-up on Strategy

As I've said earlier, there are lots of undisciplined preemptors out there. You might wonder what exactly their rationale is. It comes down to one word: frequency. By compromising their requirements, they are able to jump in immediately more often than the sound or even the light preemptor. However, there is far more uncertainty for both sides in those kinds of auctions.

I recall a hand from about seven years ago where one of my teammates opened 3♣ with a side four-card heart suit, which is usually a big no-no because you could easily be missing out on a fit in the major suit. He also had a spade void, and wanted to deprive the opponents of their bidding room. In short, his bid could have worked on certain layouts of the cards, but this was not one of them. His partner had a great hand with no club fit, and they played 3♣ going down, missing a nine-card heart fit that would have produced eleven or twelve tricks. Back in the hotel room, my teammate's decision was questioned, the consensus being that it is impossible for partner to make an accurate decision if he doesn't know what the preemptor has. His answer was 'That's right, no one knows! It turned out badly for us on this hand, but could create some positive action for us on another one.'

It's a matter of choice whether you decide to go with sound, light or undisciplined preempts, and over the years a player's feelings on the subject may change. I've moved somewhat from sound to light over the years, but never into the undisciplined school. That said, I'll readily admit that more random preempts will chalk up some notable successes to counterbalance their abject failures. The essential thing to keep in mind is that if you have a regular partner, the two of you have to come to an agreement on which style to use. Sadly, the aforementioned partnership never firmly established what road they wanted to take, and there was some consternation between them over the results from time to time. It's always important to have a shared philosophy on bidding, and especially so in the realm of competitive auctions.

QUIZ HANDS

1) Neither vulnerable, you hold:

♠ J 8 5 3 ♡ A K J 9 3 ◇ K 10 3 ♣ 5

Your RHO opens 3◇. What's your vote?

2) With your side vulnerable, the auction commences with:

West	North	East	South
pass	2♠	pass	?

Your assortment of cards is:

♠ 7 4 3 ♡ A K 6 ◇ K Q 10 7 ♣ Q 7 3

Partner shows 5-10 points with his 2♠ opening, what course should you take?

3) You're perusing this nice distributional hand with your side vulnerable:

♠ K 9 2 ♡ A K Q 7 6 3 ◇ J 8 6 5 ♣ —

Of course, the auction is at the three-level when it's your turn to speak:

West	North	East	South
		3♠	?

After you're through cursing RHO for his effrontery, you proceed with…?

4) Both sides vulnerable this time, you're looking at:

♠ A Q 4 ♡ K 7 ◇ K Q 9 7 5 ♣ A 8 4

Once again, those nasty preempts rear their ugly head, as you're faced with:

West	North	East	South
		3♣	?

What's your poison? Or do you decline to choose any beverage this time?

1)   Neither vul.

♠ J 8 5 3   ♡ A K J 9 3   ◇ K 10 3   ♣ 5

West	North	East	South
		3◇	?

Pass. This is a hand that would have opened if it was first to speak, but is not quite good enough to venture an entry into the bidding at the three-level. In order to take direct action over a preempt, you usually need a hand of 15+ points and/or a good six-card or longer suit. You have length in RHO's suit, so partner will likely reopen in some fashion in passout chair if he has any values and shortness.

The layout on this particular deal is:

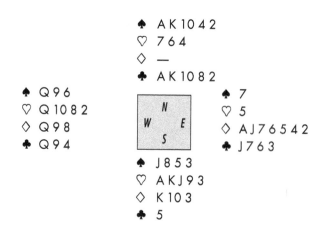

```
              ♠ A K 10 4 2
              ♡ 7 6 4
              ◇ —
              ♣ A K 10 8 2
♠ Q 9 6                        ♠ 7
♡ Q 10 8 2        N            ♡ 5
◇ Q 9 8       W       E        ◇ A J 7 6 5 4 2
♣ Q 9 4           S            ♣ J 7 6 3
              ♠ J 8 5 3
              ♡ A K J 9 3
              ◇ K 10 3
              ♣ 5
```

The trend in favor of more aggressive preemptive bidding is evidenced by the East hand — its holder might have passed rather than open 3◇ in a bygone era. However, it does meet the criteria for a preempt in that it has little if any defense outside the long suit, and with only two major-suit cards, 'getting in their faces' immediately has a lot to say for it.

Note also that if South does overcall 3♡, North is going to drive all the way to slam with three-card support, a void in diamonds, and two good suits of his own with top controls. Spades can be picked up with an accurate guess but the trumps lie badly for declarer — not an unusual occurrence when someone has announced a distributional hand.

If South passes, North can balance with 3♠ and they should end up in a spade game, which even in the worst-case scenario will lose a maximum of two or three tricks.

2)   North-South vul.

West	North	East	South
pass	2♠	pass	?

♠ 7 4 3   ♡ A K 6   ◇ K Q 10 7   ♣ Q 7 3

Since the range of a weak two-bid is generally 5-10 points, it would be precipitate to barge into game. It's worth looking for, however, and the tool you can use to find out if it has a chance is the artificial 2NT inquiry, which asks partner to describe the quality of his hand. It turns out he has:

♠ K Q 10 9 6 5   ♡ 8 7   ◇ 9 8 3   ♣ K J

and 4♠ rolls home without any trouble, losing a club and one or two diamonds. This would be the auction if the partnership used 2NT as a feature ask:

North	South
2♠	2NT
3♣*	4♠

If partner does anything other than deny a feature with 3♠, you will commit the hand to game. The 3♣ bid shows a high card in that suit, which is very good opposite your Qxx. Now there should be a reasonable play for ten tricks.

If the partnership instead uses 2NT as Ogust, we'd then have:

North	South
2♠	2NT*
3♠*	4♠

North's 3♠ shows the excellent news of a good hand along with a good suit. That will be also be sufficient for South to bid game.

3) North-South vul.

♠ K 9 2 ♡ A K Q 7 6 3 ◇ J 8 6 5 ♣ —

West	North	East	South
		3♠	?

Bid 4♡. Partner is likely short in spades and if he has some assistance in diamonds, game will have a reasonable shot. Alas, on this occasion partner indeed has a smattering of high cards, but they're not the right ones for your purposes:

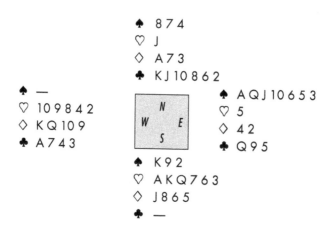

```
              ♠ 8 7 4
              ♡ J
              ◇ A 7 3
              ♣ K J 10 8 6 2
♠ —                              ♠ A Q J 10 6 5 3
♡ 10 9 8 4 2        N            ♡ 5
◇ K Q 10 9      W       E        ◇ 4 2
♣ A 7 4 3           S            ♣ Q 9 5
              ♠ K 9 2
              ♡ A K Q 7 6 3
              ◇ J 8 6 5
              ♣ —
```

West doubles 4♡ and leads the ◇K. When the smoke clears, the contract will be down two or three.

Two points are worth noting here. First, this hand is a perfect illustration of my friend's adage that 3♠ is more preemptive than 4♠. A fair number of players might well open 4♠ on these cards at favorable colors. This would leave South no choice but to pass, as either 5♡ or double is a major overbid with those cards. West and North will also pass, and North-South are now able to chalk up a plus their way. The 3♠ opening placed South on the horns of a dilemma, and he made a reasonable choice that turned out badly.

The outcome notwithstanding, you should never second-guess your decision on a hand like this. Partner had wasted values in the club suit and the same three spades you did, which is rather unlucky. There was nothing at all wrong in bidding, so don't fret too much about how this hand played out.

4)   Both vul.

♠ A Q 4   ♡ K 7   ◇ K Q 9 7 5   ♣ A 8 4

West	North	East	South
		3♣	?

Bid 3NT, applying the 'rule of 7' over enemy preempts. You are assuming partner will have about 7 of the missing HCP, and that might be sufficient to enable 3NT to make your way. Having ace-third of their suit gives you the luxury of holding up a round or two, thereby disrupting their communications. By contrast to Hand 3, the odds work out favorably for you on this layout:

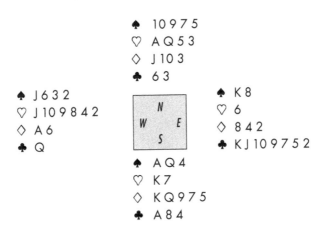

♠ 10 9 7 5
♡ A Q 5 3
◇ J 10 3
♣ 6 3

♠ J 6 3 2
♡ J 10 9 8 4 2
◇ A 6
♣ Q

♠ K 8
♡ 6
◇ 8 4 2
♣ K J 10 9 7 5 2

♠ A Q 4
♡ K 7
◇ K Q 9 7 5
♣ A 8 4

What partner has is extremely valuable, with the ◇J10x being golden and the rest of his points concentrated in the heart suit to provide your side with an additional three tricks. This time you bought the right cards with his expected assets instead of the wrong ones. Opposite this dummy, 3NT rates to take nine tricks as the preemptor will seldom have the outside ◇A.

CHAPTER 3

TWO! TWO! TWO SUITS IN ONE BID!

In bridge, new ideas in bidding come up continually. Some never gain widespread acceptance, while others gain popularity and become commonplace. A typical characteristic of a new treatment that successfully finds its way into the mainstream is that there are more frequent opportunities to use it than that which it replaced. A case in point is the negative double when partner has opened and RHO has overcalled. Responder was far more likely to be in possession of 6-11 HCP with support for the other suits than he was to have a penalty double of the overcall. Any convention that increases the number of opportunities to bid generally finds a willing audience, and so was the case with the negative double.

The same factors contributed to the acceptance of the Michaels cuebid and the Unusual 2NT. Once upon a time, in the early days of bridge, a jump overcall of 2NT after RHO's opening would show a balanced hand of 21-22 HCP with stoppers in their suit. Moreover, an immediate cuebid of opener's suit would be a hand akin to a game-forcing 2♣ opening. As you might imagine, the chance did not arise very often to trot out one of these bids as hands that powerful come up once in a blue moon, if that, once an opponent has opened the bidding. Some inventive minds suggested the idea of using each of these actions to describe hands with 5-5 or better length in two suits. Like the negative double, the idea eventually achieved a breakthrough and now most experienced partnerships use Michaels and the Unusual Notrump as a matter of course.

Two-suited overcalls are similar in their effect to preempts and weak two-bids. They also show extreme distribution, and immediately drive the auction up to the three-level if the opponents want to bid over them. The notable difference is that in a preemptive scenario the next bidder has to make his choice with no idea of what his partner has, whereas a two-suited overcall follows an opening bid, so LHO will have at least some information about partner's hand.

Two-suited overcalls have a lot going for them. With two five-card or longer suits, the chances of finding a playable trump fit are greater, and the hand can be described immediately rather than having to bid one suit and then hoping to be able to show the other conveniently later on. On the downside, two-suited overcalls can catapult your side to the three-level, which could turn out to be precariously high, and the information conveyed about the shape of the hand can be used to advantage by the opponents if they wind up as the declaring side.

Michaels

Michaels comes in two variations, depending on which suit they have opened. It always promises the unbid majors, so if they open 1♣ or 1◇, it's pretty straightforward: the cuebid shows hearts and spades. If they open a major suit, the situation isn't as clear-cut, as the overcaller now shows the other major and one of the minor suits. The following table shows how the principle works:

They Open:	You Overcall:	To Show:
1♣	2♣	hearts and spades
1◇	2◇	hearts and spades
1♡	2♡	spades and a minor
1♠	2♠	hearts and a minor

In the third and fourth auctions, since advancer may be short in the other major, there has to be a way of finding out which of the minors overcaller has. We'll explore how to do that in the section on advancing the Michaels cuebid.

THE 'MINI-MAXI' PRINCIPLE OF TWO-SUITED OVERCALLS

Most practitioners of Michaels (or the Unusual Notrump, which we'll come to shortly) use it only with hands of either:

- 10 or fewer HCP, or
- 17+ HCP and/or five or fewer losers.

With two-suiters in the vicinity of 11-16 points and 6+ losers, they will endeavor to overcall the higher-ranking suit first, and then get in the other suit at the next turn. So why bother imposing these kinds of limits on two-suited overcalls? It seems like a waste of time to use two bids to show your hand pattern when you can do it in just one shot. There are two very good reasons for breaking down the two-suited hands in this manner.

The first reason has to do with the 'two actions or one' principle. Hands with 5-5 shape and 10 or fewer points are only worth one action, so they should make the bid that immediately describes the two suits. With very strong hands, you don't mind having to go to the three-level or beyond, so it makes sense to show the two-suiter first and then continue with further action even if partner shows no signs of life.

Hands with 5-5 pattern and 11-16 points are also worth two bids, but should usually overcall the higher-ranking suit and then show the second suit at the next turn. You have enough potential ammunition to buy the contract, but no real desire to obstruct the opponents or commit to a high level in the bidding right away. If partner doesn't have enough to keep the bidding alive following an overcall, it's unlikely that you'll have missed game.

The second reason has to do with a possible high-level decision if the opponents sail to a game in their fit immediately. Now the adage 'If it isn't a good bid, it's a good sacrifice' will help you decide how to proceed. Consider as an example this bidding sequence:

LHO	Partner	RHO	You
1♡	2♡	4♡	?

They are vulnerable, you are not, and your collection of goodies is:

♠K 10 7 5   ♡8 6 3   ◇J 8 7 2   ♣A 9

Granted, you don't know which minor partner has. Regardless, since partner is outside the 11-16 range either on the high end or the low, a 4♠ bid should be automatic here. If partner has the lesser hand, 4♡ should be cold while 4♠ won't be too expensive your way and could even make on a good day. If he's got the stronger edition of Michaels, the hand definitely belongs to your side. Since your 'mini-maxi' agreement has taken the medium two-suited hands out of the equation, 4♠ will either roll home or be an excellent sacrifice more often than not.

With that agreement now in place, we can now look at some hands to decide whether or not they qualify for a Michaels cuebid. Say, for example that RHO opens 1♣:

♠KQ 9 7 6   ♡QJ 10 8 5   ◇9 4   ♣10

Yes, bid 2♣. This is a good illustration of the 'mini' version of the Michaels cuebid. The thing to remember is that it's a one-bid hand and you don't want to miss out on a heart fit by overcalling 1♠, so it's best to show both majors immediately, even if it forces partner to the two-level. As long as there's an eight-card fit in one of the suits, your side won't fare too badly.

♠ A K J 9 7 ♡ K Q J 9 2 ◇ 7 ♣ A 5

Another Michaels cuebid, this one of stronger variety. The plan here is to see which major partner opts for and then carry on to game. Sure, he might be 2-2 in the majors on a bad day, but if he has as little as three small hearts or Qx(x) in spades, a major-suit game will have decent play.

♠ A Q J 8 4 ♡ A 10 6 5 3 ◇ Q 3 ♣ 7

Overcall 1♠, and then mention the hearts at your next chance. With both major suits and a sound opening bid, there's no reason to chew up bidding space unnecessarily.

Similarly, suppose you get a 1♠ bid from RHO, and you hold:

♠ 4 ♡ K Q 8 7 6 ◇ K 7 5 4 2 ♣ A Q

On this hand 2♡ is best for the time being, as the red suits aren't good enough to commit to the three-level until you know what LHO has. If, for example, he bids 2♠ over your 2♡ and then it comes back around to you, you might consider bidding 3◇ as partner rates to have some values with their having stopped in a partscore. However, a Michaels cuebid of 2♠ crosses the Rubicon prematurely and if LHO has 10+ HCP, you'll find out quickly to your regret.

♠ 7 ♡ K J 10 7 5 ◇ A Q 9 6 3 ♣ 9 8

By contrast, this hand can venture 2♠ even with the diminished point count. With all your points appropriately located in the reds, this is a much better hand for offense, and partner should be able to make the right decision for your side.

Interlude: Support or Preference?

You've probably heard each of these terms and nodded your head because you'd feel somewhat foolish in asking their precise meaning. Here is the answer in a nutshell.

A **preference** occurs when one player has shown an unbalanced two-suiter. With minimal values, his partner has to choose between the suits without increasing the level, so may not have active (three-card or longer) support in doing so.

Support is an action that guarantees an eight-card or better trump fit. If partner goes to one of your suits voluntarily and/or with some enthusiasm, you can assume support. Here are a couple of auctions that are fairly typical in everyday bidding:

Opener	Responder
1♡	1♠
2♣	2♡

Opener	Responder
1♡	1♠
1NT	2♡

The auction on the left is a *preference* because opener has shown distaste for notrump and wants responder to choose between his two suits. The auction on the right is *support* because responder could have left opener in 1NT if he had only a doubleton heart.

You can apply the same principles to Michaels and Unusual Notrump auctions. It's very important to distinguish an auction where partner may only be giving a preference, so as to avoid getting too high. Here are a couple of tests for you:

LHO	Partner	RHO	You
		1◊	2◊
pass	2♡		

LHO	Partner	RHO	You
		1◊	2◊
pass	3♡		

With you showing at least ten major-suit cards, partner is going to choose between one of your suits and may be obliged to do so on a doubleton. His 2♡ in the first auction may be only two trumps. What else can he do with a hand like:

♠ 5   ♡ Q 6   ◊ Q 10 9 2   ♣ J 9 7 5 4 2

Now take the second auction. The action of *jumping* to the three-level, when he could have just bid 2♡ instead, now confirms actual support and at least mild game interest. Partner's hand could be

♠ K 4   ♡ J 8 5 4   ◊ A J 7 2   ♣ 9 8 4

ADVANCING A MICHAELS CUEBID

When partner trots out a Michaels cuebid over a minor-suit opening, you can determine right away which of your high cards are apt to be useful — you know exactly which two suits he has. With a decent fit and cards that known to be 'working', take some kind of encouraging action, jumping a level in one of partner's suits or even to game if the hand justifies it. Above all, remember that bidding one of those suits at the cheapest level will be interpreted as a minimal preference and you won't hear again from partner unless he has the 'maxi' hand.

Normally, even if overcaller has the 'mini' or weaker hand, he won't exceed six or seven losers, so think in terms of game with the ability to cover three or more of them if you like one of partner's suits. If you have a fit for both suits or can recognize that there will be a nine-card or longer trump combination, you can be more aggressive yet. Conversely, with a minimal fit and a shortage of guaranteed tricks, you'll pull in your horns and not offer any encouragement. Some examples will illustrate how to proceed:

LHO	Partner	RHO	You
1◇	2◇	pass	?

♠ K 6 4 ♡ 7 2 ◇ K Q 4 ♣ J 9 6 3 2

Bid 2♠ only. With partner having a shortage of minor-suit cards, the ◇KQ may not be particularly valuable. If he can't take a further move, you won't be missing game.

♠ A J 8 ♡ K 5 ◇ J 7 5 4 ♣ 10 9 6 3

Same eight-card fit, and identical point count, but a lot more appealing with the extra spade honor and the king of partner's other long suit, hearts. I'd jump to 3♠ here, as game is possible opposite even a decent 'mini' hand.

♠ Q 7 3 ♡ A J 6 5 3 ◇ J 9 4 2 ♣ 8

With a ten-card fit, the trick-taking potential of this hand increases vastly. Every value has good potential, from the ♠Q all the way to the singleton club. It makes sense to bash right into 4♡ because it will make a fair amount of the time and also because they have a great club fit that you want to prevent them from discovering.

When partner has used Michaels over the opponent's major-suit opening, the environment is murkier since only one of his suits is known. If advancer has three or more of the unbid major, he has an immediate fit. With no fit for the major, but three or more of each minor, he needs to ask what the Michaels bidder's other suit is so as to play in his minor. A 2NT bid is one way you can ask for partner's other suit. Partner then bids his minor as cheaply as possible, and can only jump in his minor suit if he has the 'maxi' hand. Since that's quite a mouthful, let's look at some examples:

LHO	Partner	RHO	You
1♡	2♡	pass	?

♠KQ87 ♡10865 ◊A4 ♣Q93

Only 11 HCP but a hand that should jump to 4♠, with a guaranteed nine-card fit and one sure trick outside in the ◊A. It doesn't matter what partner's minor is, because you have an additional useful value in either the ♣Q or the doubleton diamond.

♠2 ♡QJ75 ◊A103 ♣J10854

Here you'd like to find out what partner's other suit is since there is no fit in spades. Advancer uses 2NT as the mechanism to ask which minor overcaller has. You expect it to be diamonds, but you never know, he might surprise you and bid clubs. At any rate, you'll end up playing in a minor suit as that is the only eight-card or better fit your side has available.

♠7 ♡AJ105 ◊86 ♣KQJ952

Bid 3♣. By not asking with 2NT, advancer is more or less insisting on clubs as the trump suit and does not want to hear about overcaller's minor if it's diamonds. The Michaels cuebidder should understand that he's being overruled and not engage in a trump fight.

RESPONDING TO PARTNER'S OPENING AFTER A MICHAELS CUEBID

A Michaels cuebid by the opponents gets the bidding up to a high level fairly quickly, and advertises wild distribution and possible unfavorable splits. Hands of 6 to a bad 8 HCP should therefore generally pass. With a decent 8 to 10 HCP and adequate support, you can raise partner's suit as cheaply as possible. With 11+ points (or a juicy 10), decide in which category the hand belongs:

1) A good fit for opener's suit and no strong desire to penalize the opponents.
2) No proven fit and the ability to defend one or both of their suits.
3) No support for partner or inclination to defend their suits, but five or more cards in a 'new' suit, i.e. one not specifically promised by the opponents.

Now let's take these three situations in reverse order. With type 3, responder simply bids his long suit. With a hand that falls into category 2, he doubles the cuebid, to see where the opponents are going to scurry to, and then decides whether to double or bid at that point.

With type 1, the supporting hand, you can show game interest via a cuebid of one of RHO's suits. It's important, though, to identify what the 'Promised Land', or most likely game contract, is. If partner has opened a major suit, you'll be looking for game in his suit. If he's opened a minor suit, the ideal game contract would be 3NT provided that your side has both of their suits adequately stopped. With that in mind, we are ready to look at the following table:

We Open:	They Bid:	Our 'Promised Land' If We Have Support Is:	The Cuebid Means:
1♣	2♣ (majors)	3NT, if possible, otherwise partscore or game in opener's minor	11+ points with support and a stopper in the bid suit. A bid of 2♡ means a heart stopper, 2♠ means a spade stopper.
1♢	2♢ (majors)	same as above	same as above
1♡	2♡ (spades and a minor)	4♡	A bid of 2♠, their only known suit, is a limit raise or better in hearts. It says nothing about spades as you are trying for game in hearts rather than notrump.
1♠	2♠ (hearts and a minor)	4♠	A bid of 3♡, their known suit, is a spade raise with at least a good 10 HCP.

Now for some examples of the above chart in action:

Partner	♠ A J 6　♡ 7 4　♢ A 10 9 6 5　♣ Q J 9

You	♠ 10 4　♡ K J 10　♢ K Q 7 2　♣ A 10 5 3

LHO	Partner	RHO	You
	1♢	2♢	2♡
pass	2NT	pass	3NT
all pass			

When partner opens, you want to be in game, but after the Michaels cuebid on your right, stoppers in both their suits are required to arrive at 3NT. With a heart stopper and diamond support, bid 2♡. Opener, with a high card in spades, can now bid 2NT, and you'll sail into game.

Partner	♠ A 10 8 6 5　♡ K 9 4　♢ A J 6　♣ 7 5

You	♠ K J 4　♡ 7 2　♢ Q 8 5 2　♣ K Q 6 4

LHO	Partner	RHO	You
	1♠	2♠	3♡
pass	3♠	all pass	

With 11 HCP, you have too good a hand for a raise to 3♠, but not quite enough to force to game. These values can be shown with a cuebid of their known suit, 3♡. Opener has a minimum (the ♡K is now of dubious value), and therefore declines the game invitation with 3♠.

The Unusual 2NT (U2)

The Unusual 2NT, like the Michaels cuebid, shows a two-suited hand, 5-5 or better. Which two suits? The premise is that overcaller will be advertising the two *lowest unbid* suits. To become familiar with the gist of it, you can refer to the chart below:

They Open:	Partner Bids:	To Show:
1♣	2NT	diamonds and hearts
1♢	2NT	clubs and hearts
1♡	2NT	the minors, clubs and diamonds
1♠	2NT	the minors again, the lowest unbid suits

For the most part, the guidelines for the usage of the U2 (my nickname for the Unusual 2NT) are similar to those I've recommended for Michaels, since they are birds of the same feather in terms of the expected distribution. However, there are slight but important differences, which may help the memory process as you venture into the territory of two-suited overcalls.

First, with the U2, the suits are always known, as you can see from the above chart. That's only partially the case in Michaels, where you know both suits if the opening bid is a minor, but only one suit (the other major) if the opening bid is 1♡ or 1♠.

Second, the U2 always *denies* spades, the highest-ranked suit. By contrast, unless they have opened 1♠, the Michaels cuebidder will always *have* spades as one of his suits. In any competitive auction, if the high-card values are roughly equal between the two sides, whoever has a fit in the master suit will likely end up declaring the hand. You'll find, therefore, that in a Michaels auction you'll have a better shot of winning the honors. However, with the U2, your side will be playing the hand only if you have them outgunned in high-card values or are taking a sacrifice against a game they've bid.

Let's do our usual run-through on whether or not to sally forth with the immediate two-suited bid:

LHO	Partner	RHO	You
		1♣	?

♠ J ♡ K J 9 6 4 ◇ K Q 8 7 6 ♣ 6 2

Bid 2NT to show the lowest unbid suits, hearts and diamonds. With 9 HCP and a hand suited mainly for offense, you want to get both suits in right away as you're only worth a single action. The U2 also has the benefit of giving them a tougher path to reach spades at the appropriate level.

♠ A 7 ♡ A Q 10 6 5 ◇ Q J 8 4 3 ♣ 9

Here a 1♡ overcall is the way to go. With an unbalanced 13 HCP, the hand is worth two bids. It also has enough defensive potential that you don't have to be in such a hurry to obstruct them in the auction.

WHATCHA GONNA DO WHEN THE OPPONENTS' U2 RUNS WILD ON YOU?

When the opponents butt in with the Unusual 2NT, responder only has the three-level available to describe his hand. With 6 or 7 points, he will normally pass. Decent support and 8-10 points is enough to muster up a raise to the three-level.

That leaves us with the task of how to proceed with the better hands of 11+ points after a minor-suit opening and a U2 bid by your adversaries. I'll set up a table that revisits the 'Promised Land' concept of possible games for us to strive for:

We Open:	They Bid:	To Show:	Our Promised Land:
1♣	2NT	Diamonds & hearts	4♠ if we have a fit there, 3NT otherwise
1◇	2NT	Clubs & hearts	Same as above

Because they've denied spades, we'll be looking for a fit and possibly game in that suit; failing that, responder can try for 3NT or suggest defending their eventual contract. Here is the checklist for his actions and what they mean:

3 of opener's minor	Four- or five-card support, 8-9 points.
3♠	Five+ spades, 11+ points.
Cuebid of one of their suits	Support for opener's minor, high card in the bid suit, 11+ points, trying for 3NT.
Double	11+ points, denies spade length or good support for opener's minor. Suggests defending whatever landing spot they touch down in.

You'll notice that I haven't addressed what to do as responder when partner opens 1♡ or 1♠ and they interfere with 2NT. That's because it gets a tad more complicated and I intend to cover that in a later chapter when I describe the 'Unusual vs. Unusual' convention.

QUIZ HANDS

1) With neither side vulnerable, you're dealt these tickets:

♠ Q 10 5 4 ♡ A 9 ◇ A J 9 4 ♣ J 7 3

Partner opens, but they naturally just won't let your side have a free run:

West	North	East	South
	1♣	2NT	?

RHO's 2NT shows the two lower unbid suits, diamonds and hearts. So whatcha gonna do?

2) Both sides vulnerable, you hold:

♠ Q ♡ A 5 ◇ A Q 9 2 ♣ Q 6 5 4 3 2

West	North	East	South
1♣	2NT	pass	?

Diamonds and hearts again with partner's U2. So what should the outlook be on this hand?

3) You now have, with neither side vulnerable:

♠ — ♡ K J 9 5 2 ◇ A 6 ♣ A J 9 8 7 3

The auction commences with:

West	North	East	South
		1♠	?

How to proceed? Michaels 2♠, or 2♣ followed by bidding the hearts later on?

4) And to conclude, neither side vulnerable as you're looking at:

♠Q 10 8 4 ♡J 5 4 ◇A 10 ♣K J 9 3

A balanced 11-count, and by the time it rolls around to you the auction has gone:

West	North	East	South
pass	1♠	2♠	?

RHO is showing hearts and a minor. What action should you take?

1) Neither vul.

♠ Q 10 5 4   ♡ A 9   ◇ A J 9 4   ♣ J 7 3

West	North	East	South
	1♣	2NT	⁇

RHO is showing the red suits, diamonds and hearts, with his 2NT overcall. So what is your plan going to be?

One alternative is to bid 3NT, as you have enough points for that contract to have a good play. However, you might be able to get an even better result by doubling wherever they go to. You have the diamonds locked up, and if partner has some heart length, they might not have a safe haven there, either. Start off by doubling 2NT, to show 11+ HCP and interest in defending. If they go to hearts, you hope partner can double. If he can't, you can then bid 3NT. In essence, 3NT is your fallback position if you can't profitably double their contract, but in the meantime, you at least give yourself the chance of nailing their hides to the wall. And sure enough, Christmas will come early for your side this time:

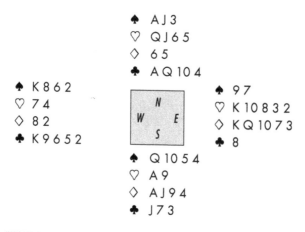

<pre>
              ♠ A J 3
              ♡ Q J 6 5
              ◇ 6 5
              ♣ A Q 10 4
♠ K 8 6 2   ♠ 9 7
♡ 7 4   N   ♡ K 10 8 3 2
◇ 8 2   W   E   ◇ K Q 10 7 3
♣ K 9 6 5 2   S   ♣ 8
              ♠ Q 10 5 4
              ♡ A 9
              ◇ A J 9 4
              ♣ J 7 3
</pre>

West	North	East	South
	1♣	2NT	dbl
pass	pass	3◇	dbl
all pass			

With identical red-suit holdings, West passes the double to let the U2 overcaller choose. Declarer will lose a club, two spades, three diamonds and two or three hearts, for at least down four. Perfect defense can hold him to four tricks for +1100, but even +800 will be a far better score for your side than +460 in 3NT.

2) Both vul.

♠ Q ♡ A 5 ◇ A Q 9 2 ♣ Q 6 5 4 3 2

West	North	East	South
1♣	2NT	pass	?

This hand is nothing short of awesome with partner showing diamonds and hearts with his U2. The diamond and heart values will solidify the red suits, and with your shortness in the other major, there rate to be only two black-suit losers, if that. You should bid 5◇, expecting it to make, and come up roses, as the hands are:

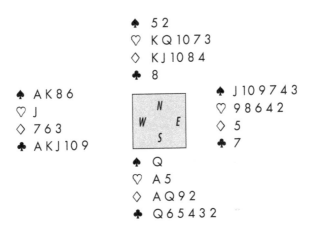

Making 5◇ is no problem, losing just a club and a spade. The other benefit you achieve from getting there right away is freezing the opponents out of their ten-card spade fit since East, with just a paltry jack, didn't have the values to mention them. The U2 ran into a buzzsaw on Hand 1, but leads to an awesome result here.

3) Neither vul.

♠ — ♡ K J 9 5 2 ◇ A 6 ♣ A J 9 8 7 3

To use Michaels or to overcall clubs and then bid hearts, that is the question. Is this hand a 'maxi'? To qualify, it should be 17+ points or no worse than five losers. You have just 13 HCP, but only five losers (two each in hearts and clubs plus a diamond), so the hand barely comes in as a high-end Michaels.

There is another key reason for showing both suits immediately. The opponents have spades, the master suit, and your void suggests they might go places there in a hurry. Because you might not have the luxury of mentioning the hearts at a convenient level, you should bring the other major into the picture as quickly as possible with 2♠. The four hands in this instance are:

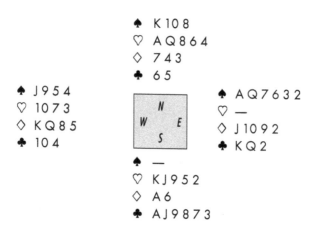

When this deal occurred, the bidding went:

West	North	East	South
		1♠	2♣
2♠	pass	4♠	5♣
pass	pass	dbl	all pass

At the table, South overcalled 2♣ and West had just enough to raise to 2♠. Opener went on to game and now overcaller was faced with an uncomfortable choice: repeat the clubs and bury the heart suit, or bid 5♥ and maybe have to go to the six-level if partner had to retreat to clubs. South opted for 5♣, which lost two clubs and a diamond.

This would be the Michaels auction:

West	North	East	South
		1♠	2♠
pass	4♥	all pass	

Note how the Michaels cuebid changes things entirely. West lacks the stuff to go to the three-level and passes. North jumps to 4♥, knowing his side has a ten-card fit, and opener cannot really contest the auction further. Even if he does bid 4♠, South will forge on to 5♡, which can make eleven tricks.

4) Neither vul.

♠ Q 10 8 4   ♡ J 5 4   ◇ A 10   ♣ K J 9 3

West	North	East	South
pass	1♠	2♠	?

As responder, you're in a bit of a pinch. If you compete with a raise to 3♠, opener will expect you to have 8-10 points. While it's a decent hand, it's not quite worth driving all the way to game. How do you show 11-12 points? Since they've cuebid opener's suit and made life difficult, you can bid 3♡, their known suit, to promise support and better than a single raise. If North has a minimum, he'll sign off in 3♠, but if he's got extras, he'll bid game. The layout this time is:

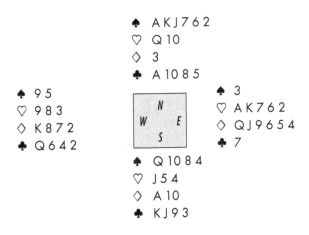

```
                    ♠  A K J 7 6 2
                    ♡  Q 10
                    ◇  3
                    ♣  A 10 8 5
    ♠  9 5                              ♠  3
    ♡  9 8 3          N                 ♡  A K 7 6 2
    ◇  K 8 7 2    W        E            ◇  Q J 9 6 5 4
    ♣  Q 6 4 2        S                 ♣  7
                    ♠  Q 10 8 4
                    ♡  J 5 4
                    ◇  A 10
                    ♣  K J 9 3
```

Opener will gladly bid 4♠, which makes in comfort. West is unlikely to compete to the five-level, although a feisty East might press on. Even if they do find the paying sacrifice, North will most likely continue on to the five-level, and the location of the ♣Q is marked with the red suits known to be on declarer's left.

CHAPTER 4

BIDDING AS THE AUCTION PROGRESSES

In the first three chapters, we've talked about general principles of entering the bidding in direct seat when the opponents have been the first ones in. The three basic tools of competitive bidding were described: the takeout double, the overcall and the negative double. We then added preemptive bids and two-suited overcalls to our toolkit.

The focus now moves to situations where there has been more action on the bidding front. After an opening bid and takeout double, does anything change for responder in how to show his hand? If there has already been an opening bid and a response, what do you need to come in? Another common scenario is where the enemy bidding has petered out and you have to decide whether it's advisable to sell out. To borrow the title of a Tom Cruise movie, this can be risky business. However, most of us who have played this game for a while realize that while the meek could inherit the earth, they are not apt to garner many victories at the bridge table. The problem is to distinguish hands on which bidding constitutes an acceptable risk from those where charging in rates to lead to a dismal result.

In the Sandwich Position: What to Do?

You've probably heard the expression 'sandwich position' used in bridge lingo. It refers to auctions that have started with an opening bid on your left and a response on your right — you have not yet had a chance to make a call, but are sandwiched between two opponents who have bid. The opponents are guaranteed to have at least 18 HCP (12 + 6) and potentially a lot more. Because of the values they are known to have, entering the fray requires assets that will stave off disaster if partner has very little to offer in the way of help. Having strong distributional features in the hand is a must, particularly if your contemplated action will push the level higher. Let's take a look at some hands and decide if they merit some activity on our part. So far the bidding has gone:

West	North	East	South
1♣	pass	1♡	?

♠AQJ96 ♡A83 ◇1095 ♣62

I'd bid 1♠ here, especially at matchpoints, since it has two advantages. First, you'd very much like a spade lead from partner. Second, because you're in possession of the master suit, you may be able to buy the partscore or at least nudge them to the three-level.

♠Q9754 ♡K6 ◇A82 ♣Q76

Same 11 points, but this hand should refrain from immediate action. The holdings in both their suits are unappetizing. Moreover, you don't have a crying need for a spade lead. Suppose they wind up in a notrump contract and partner obediently leads spades from his doubleton when his normal lead was a diamond from his ◇K10xxx? He likely won't be a happy camper once all is said and done.

♠5 ♡K962 ◇AK10974 ♣82

Bid 2◇. You have some hope of making it if partner has a few of them, and the suit is good enough that you aren't likely to get doubled. The distribution is more attractive than either of the first two hands, and that's reason enough to justify the entry at a higher level.

If you have both of the unbid suits along with decent values and/or shape, it can often be right to compete in the sandwich position. Here is a new auction and a pair of hands to illustrate:

West	North	East	South
1◇	pass	1♠	?

♠A4 ♡AJ95 ◇82 ♣QJ865

♠9 ♡KJ764 ◇87 ♣KQ965

The first one is straightforward, as you can double — takeout for hearts and clubs. The second hand has slightly better distribution but a takeout double, even in sandwich position, should have a couple of defensive tricks.

With only 9 HCP, the hand isn't worth two bids, either, so overcalling hearts and then mentioning clubs later isn't really a valid option. The solution is to dispense with a 1NT overcall as showing a balanced 15-18 and use it to show a distributional takeout for the other two suits, promising good shape but not guaranteeing a world of high card points. This convention is called the 'Sandwich Notrump'. It's a treatment that is gaining in popularity, since the 5-5 two-suiter will likely occur more frequently than the balanced strong hand.

You might find these useful guidelines for deciding whether to make your presence felt when both opponents have bid:

- Sandwich position actions demand distributional security because it's dangerous to step in when there has been an opening bid and response (and *neither* opponent has yet limited his hand).
- It's preferable to have 5-4 shape for a takeout double. You'd need a mighty fine hand to contemplate an entry into the bidding with 4-4 in the unbid suits and balanced distribution.
- Overcalls at *any* level require quality suits. One-level actions can be made on more balanced hands if the suit is up to snuff. Not so for two-level overcalls, for which you should have a six-card suit or its equivalent.
- *Convention Alert!* Use a 'Sandwich' 1NT overcall, showing 5-5 or better in the unbid suits and less than opening values.

TWO BIDS OR ONE? A SECOND LOOK

It might be helpful to revisit one of the topics from Chapter 1 and see how it can also be an aid in determining your action in the sandwich position. As I've mentioned previously, any competitive decision should be based on how many actions your hand is worth. Suppose you are faced with this start to the bidding:

LHO	Partner	RHO	You
1♣	pass	1♡	?

Now we can think about the following hands and select the appropriate option.

♠A K 10 5 4   ♡A 9   ◇J 7 3 2   ♣8 4

Two bids or one? Definitely only one. Overcall 1♠ — even though you have four diamonds, it's more crucial to introduce the decent five-card spade suit while you have the chance.

♠AK65 ♡8 ◇AKJ764 ♣103

This one? You're going to compete vigorously, bidding twice if necessary even if the second action has to be at the three-level. How do you get the ball rolling? Much of effective bidding is the principle of anticipation. This hand should double first, and then bid diamonds. Now an accurate picture has been conveyed — four spades along with five or six diamonds. That way, you'll never have to increase the level to play your best fit.

♠AQJ7 ♡6 ◇K86543 ♣95

Is this a one or two bid hand? Just one, as the hand isn't quite worth another salvo. What action to take? Go with the takeout double. The spades are too good not to bring into the picture.

Free Bids in Competition

What's your reaction upon hearing the expression 'free bid' in the conversations of the more experienced players? It would be nice to get a clarification on the topic, but perhaps you were too shy to ask. Even if you did, the answer might not have been particularly enlightening. Here, then is the scoop on what it's all about.

A **free bid** is a voluntary action when RHO has intervened. You are no longer forced to bid, even if you would have been without RHO's action, since partner will now have another kick at the can if you pass. There are many scenarios of this type, but for the purposes of the current discussion, we'll be referring specifically to auctions where you have opened, partner has responded, and RHO has competed.

- Free bids that do *not* require opener to have significant extras:
  » A raise of partner's suit to the two-level.
  » A rebid of your own suit at the two-level (promises six or more of them).
  » 1NT (should have two stoppers in their suit).

- Free bids that should have extra values:
  » A bid of a new suit.
  » 2NT (whether or not it's a jump).
  » Any three-level bid.

For these purposes, a minimum hand would be 12-14 balanced, and/or 7-8 losers, whereas 'extras' would be 15+ HCP and/or 5-6 losers.

So much for the general theory of it. Now we can take a look at some actual hands and determine whether they meet the criteria listed above:

LHO	Partner	RHO	You
			1♣
pass	1♡	1♠	?

♠AJ9 ♡K107 ◇1042 ♣AJ106

While the hand is a minimum opener, it has potentially two spade stoppers and it also has three cards and a couple of honors in partner's suit. There is a fair amount of trick-taking potential in both his suit and yours, so it would be quite all right to make the 'free' 1NT rebid here.

♠Q852 ♡Q6 ◇AQ9 ♣K754

This 13-count pales by comparison in several respects. You have just one spade stopper and a lesser holding in responder's suit; besides that, your own suit is nothing to write home about. With this unappetizing collection, the best thing to do is pass for now and see whether partner has enough values to act at his turn.

LHO	Partner	RHO	You
			1◇
pass	1♡	2♣	?

♠A74 ♡A10 ◇KQ9743 ♣64

While this hand is minimum pointwise, it definitely has its good qualities: it contains a nice-looking six-card suit and fast tricks outside. That qualifies it for a free 2◇ bid.

♠KJ2 ♡A8 ◇Q76542 ♣Q3

Here your 12-point opening has gone downhill with RHO's 2♣ overcall, which turns your ♣Qx into a dubious value. On this hand, there's not the same urgency to repeat a broken diamond suit, even with length. If partner isn't able to squeak in passout chair, the hand likely doesn't belong to your side.

LHO	Partner	RHO	You
			1♣
pass	1♠	2♡	?

♠7 ♡94 ◇A K 10 3 ♣A Q J 8 3 2

This hand is 'only' 14 HCP, but contains extras in trick-taking ability. The loser-count is a mere five (one spade, two hearts and a trick each in diamonds and clubs). You should therefore have no qualms in rebidding 3♣ freely.

♠K ♡9 4 2 ◇A Q 4 ♣A J 6 5 3 2

This assortment, however, does not merit a free 3♣ bid, as your long suit is weaker and you now have seven losers. If you plunge in with a bid and responder settles in 3NT, he isn't going to be impressed with the quality of your suit and the shortage of working high-card values. So pass and await further developments. If your side belongs in the auction, partner will muster up a bid at his turn.

Responding to Partner's Opening Bid after a Takeout Double

After partner's opening bid and a takeout double on your right, a fair number of things remain the same but some new options present themselves too. Here's the basic framework:

- New suits are a one-round force, just as if RHO had passed.
- Single raises remain 6-9 points.
- The 1NT response gets a slight boost, and is now 8 to a bad 10 HCP.
- Two actions change significantly:
  - » A jump raise is no longer 10-11 — it becomes a weak, distributional raise with lots of trumps and not many points.
  - » A 2NT response over the double now takes on an artificial meaning, and shows a limit raise or better in opener's suit. Typically, it promises extra trump length and/or shortness somewhere.

I'll discuss these more fully and explain the rationale for this change in the bidding landscape in Chapter 7, as this structure is now rapidly becoming the norm with most partnerships.

- The new kid on the block is the redouble. It always shows at least 10 points of fair quality. Since responder hasn't used the conventional 2NT bid to show a decent hand with support, he is denying a great fit with opener and suggesting that penalizing the opponents' eventual contract might be a viable option for his side.

Having described the options, we can now move on to what you should do as responder, depending on how strong a hand you have:

- With 6-7 HCP, you should bid only if you have support for opener's suit *or* a five-card major of your own that can be shown at the one-level. Otherwise, you are best off passing.
- With 8-9 points, it's business as usual. With a four-card or longer major that you can show at the one-level, bid it. Failing that, you can raise opener with adequate support or venture 1NT.
- With a decent 10 or more points, you can do one of three things:
  - » With primary support for opener and no real interest in defending, jump to 2NT, showing a limit raise or better of opener's suit.
  - » With a 5-5 two-suiter or a long suit of 6+ cards, make a forcing bid in a new suit.
  - » With anything else, including a balanced hand with three-card support for opener's major, redouble. As we'll see in Chapter 6, the partnership is now committed to further action regardless of where the opponents go.

We can now apply these principles to the following array of hands, with the bidding thus far having gone:

LHO	Partner	RHO	You
	1◇	dbl	?

♠AJ876 ♡64 ◇752 ♣Q108

Bid 1♠. Only 7 HCP, but the five-card major makes it just worth a response once RHO has doubled.

♠984 ♡Q976 ◇J63 ♣K82

Pass. A bid of 1♡ over the double would be a one-round force and might get your side too high. The chances of a 4-4 heart fit have diminished as RHO's action has implied that suit. If opener can't bid again, your side will be outgunned pointwise.

♠A43 ♡KJ107 ◇J65 ♣875

Bid 1♡. With a 9-count, your side is now certain to have the majority of the points and that's reason enough to mention the hearts over the double.

♠K4 ♡QJ8 ◇1062 ♣Q10743

Since this hand is in the 8-9 range, it should take a bid. With no major-suit length, you should respond 1NT just as you would have if RHO had passed.

♠J73 ♡86 ◇K1054 ♣KJ76

Bid 2◇. Yes, it's possible opener might only have three of them. However, with 8 HCP, you again have the values to bid, and which is more descriptive of your hand — a 1NT bid with the shabby major-suit holdings, or a raise of partner's minor? I think most experts would vote for the raise.

♠AQ ♡J94 ◇K953 ♣Q542

Redouble. The artificial 2NT raise should promise five diamonds, since opener might only have three of them. You can raise diamonds next time around unless partner doubles their contract in the meantime.

Third-Seat Openings

If you haven't done so already, you are certainly going to run into opponents (and maybe partners) who will open light in third seat, perhaps with as few as 8-10 HCP. In doing so, they are presuming that the opponent in fourth chair is about to open and they want to cause trouble by getting in first.

Opening in third seat on marginal hands can be effective if done properly, but it also poses a couple of major headaches for a partnership. The first is that responder often pulls in his horns too much worrying that partner is super-light and game can be missed as a result.

The other thing to keep in mind is that a third-seat opener should have some useful purpose in mind. His hand should be good enough either to have a chance to buy the contract or to position his side to defend in optimum fashion should the opponents end up declaring.

The principles I follow in third seat are these:

- With a good 13 or more HCP, I'll open the same thing I would have in first or second chair.

- With 10 to a bad 13 points, I tend to open the suit I want led, even if it's only a four-card major.
- I don't normally open 8- or 9-point hands in third chair, but if I do, it will be on a good five-card or longer suit *and* an unbalanced hand. Opening extremely light on balanced hands is not a recipe for success.

Keeping these guidelines in mind, we can now tackle some hands that came up in actual play, with you being in third seat after two passes:

♠ 6   ♡ A Q 10 7   ◇ A Q 9   ♣ J 8 5 4 2

Open 1♡. *Someone* is going to bid spades. If it's the opponents, you'd like to be suggesting a heart rather than a club lead. If it's partner responding in the suit, you want to be in a position to show both of your suits conveniently. If you elected to open 1♣ instead, you're not going to be overly thrilled with your rebid choices after partner bids 1♠.

♠ K J 10 8 3   ♡ 8   ◇ J 7 3   ♣ A 10 9 2

Although you only have a 9-count, a third-seat 1♠ is worth considering, especially if you are not vulnerable. It prevents the opponents from getting in the heart suit cheaply, and because you have the ability to play in three suits, you can cope with any response by partner other than 2♡.

♠ 7 5   ♡ A Q 10 3 2   ◇ K 4 2   ♣ 10 6 5

It's best to pass on this one. A third-seat opening is only in the ballgame if you can handle most of the likely responses. Some might be tempted to open 1♡, but what if partner bids 1♠? Leaving him in what might be a 4-2 fit is out of the question, but if you rebid 1NT, he'll then expect legitimate opening values and carry your side beyond its depth.

I'll come back to responding to third-seat openings in a later chapter and discuss the various forms of the Drury convention. The focus here was to identify what types of hands with less than full values are appropriate for a third-seat opening. We'll save the additional bells and whistles for later.

Balancing — An Overview

While balancing is similar to competing immediately, the requirements for taking this sort of action are not quite so demanding. The opponents have ground to a halt without showing any game ambitions so there is a measure of safety from that fact alone. While it's seldom right to act in direct chair without an unbalanced hand of some kind, you'll frequently do it in passout seat.

Effective balancing is an art, and I want to make one thing perfectly clear. If you've failed to consider your options well in advance of the bidding being passed around to you, and find yourself hemming and hawing about whether or not to jump in, your best course is to pass, especially if you are up against strong opponents. They can sniff any doubt or reluctance on your part, draw the correct inference from it, and make you pay accordingly. Suppose you are greeted with this auction:

LHO	Partner	RHO	You
1◇	pass	1♡	pass
2♡	pass	pass	?

and your hand is:

♠ Q 7 5   ♡ J 4 3   ◇ A 6   ♣ K J 9 6 4

With balanced distribution and a mediocre suit, the hand wasn't worth an immediate 2♣ overcall. The opponents have now screeched to a halt in 2♡, and you can safely assume that partner has just one or two of them, plus around 7-10 HCP. The chances are reasonable that you have an eight-card fit of your own in the club suit, and it might pay off to wade in at this point, as you could either buy the contract and make it, or nudge them beyond their depth to 3♡.

However, any balancing notions should have started at the very moment your LHO raised to 2♡. From that point on, you should have been weighing the pros and cons of backing into the auction and been ready to make your decision *in tempo* once it got passed around to you. If instead you put your thoughts in neutral and only began to contemplate action when your RHO passed, you are now at a disadvantage because the opponents are now perfectly aware that you don't have a clear-cut bid. In the words of the Boy Scout motto, 'Be Prepared' when you're faced with a balancing decision.

With that advice in mind, we can now move on to identify the most common balancing scenarios, and which ones are the safest for getting into the auction. We'll start with when a one-level opening gets passed around to you, as this is probably the safest of all auctions in which to compete, even with a modest hand. The only way you might possibly get burned is if opener has a powerful two-suiter and catches a fit in his other suit when you could have passed him out. That, however, will be a rare occurrence.

Remember that it doesn't mean partner has a poor hand just because he has not competed right away. He could either have a 'trap pass' with length in the enemy suit, or a decent hand that simply didn't have an appealing bid.

This is typical of situations where a failure to balance can lead to a heated exchange between partners:

You: ♠ J 4   ♡ K J 3   ◇ A J 8 6   ♣ K 9 8 2

Partner: ♠ A 10 9 7   ♡ 6 5   ◇ K 7 5 3   ♣ Q 10 6

LHO	Partner	RHO	You
		1♡	pass
pass	pass		

And the conversation goes:

You: My, what a splendid result! Plus 50 against 1♡ when we can take ten tricks in diamonds or eight to nine tricks in notrump. Did someone take all the red cards out of your bidding box, partner?

Partner: I only had 9 points, for crying out loud! If I dared take a bid on this pile of junk as an unpassed hand, I'd never hear the end of it! You couldn't muster up a bid on full opening values?

You: What, pray tell? Make a takeout double and hear you bid some number of spades opposite my doubleton jack? Overcall one of my sketchy four-card suits? Oh, I get it, you want me to bid 1NT on my 13-count. Or maybe the unusual 2NT on my 4-4 in the minors. Am I getting warm yet?

Partner: Yeah, I can see what you mean. Nothing really stands out with that hand, does it? And I have enough support for the unbid suits to reopen with a double when 1♡ gets passed around to me, I suppose. But what's to stop you from jumping to 3NT with that 13-count?

You: If we decide to allow a reopening double with as few as 9-10 points, then maybe if I bid 1NT over it, that should be 8-11, and then a jump to 2NT shows a minimum opening hand of 12-14 HCP. Then I won't be punishing you for a balancing action.

Partner: Okay, I can see doing it that way. I don't think we'll have a repeat of that fiasco now that we've had a chance to discuss it.

BIDDING OVER AN *UNPASSED* PARTNER'S BALANCING DOUBLE

Here's what you would bid over a direct takeout double:

LHO	Partner	RHO	You
1♡	dbl	pass	?

Partner will have at least opening values, so:

1♠, 2♣, 2◇	0 to a bad 8 HCP.
1NT	8-10 with stopper(s) in hearts.
2♠, 3♣, 3◇	Good 8 to 11 HCP.
2NT	11-12 with stopper(s) in hearts.

And here's how things change to accommodate partner's possibly reduced values for a balancing double:

LHO	Partner	RHO	You
		1♡	pass
pass	dbl	pass	?

While partner is unlimited, he could have as few as 9-10 HCP, so:

1♠, 2♣, 2◇	0 to a bad 9 HCP.
1NT	Good 9 to 11 with stopper(s) in hearts.
2♠, 3♣, 3◇	10 to 12 HCP (9 with a five-card suit would also suffice).
2NT	12-13 with stopper(s) in hearts.

As you can see, the theme when partner doubles in balancing seat is that we add a couple of points to the jumps. This gives us a margin of safety since he might have a bit less than opening values.

BALANCING WITH NOTRUMP

We can now look at another balancing option, using the same auction as before:

LHO	Partner	RHO	You
1♡	pass	pass	?

You have a fairly decent hand:

♠K6 ♡AJ8 ◇KQ73 ♣10964

Once RHO passes, the odds are very good that your side has the majority of high cards and could even be in the game zone. You hardly want to sell out meekly to 1♡, but you don't have a five-card suit to bid or enough spades to make a takeout double. You can resolve the dilemma of how best to get into the bidding by establishing this simple agreement with partner:

- In direct seat, play strong notrump overcalls
- In passout chair, use weak notrump overcalls and decide on the exact range.

Now let's talk about stoppers in the enemy suit. If LHO has opened a major, hearts or spades, he has at least five of them and is apt to lead them. You therefore need high cards in their suit to proceed with a balancing 1NT.

If, on the other hand, LHO has opened a minor, he might only have three or four of them. Having a stopper, while certainly desirable, is not as essential as it would be if they open in a major. Suppose the bidding goes:

LHO	Partner	RHO	You
1◇	pass	pass	?

and you have this hand to mull over:

♠K2 ♡AQ7 ◇10865 ♣A1063

You can't double because you don't have support for the majors. Yet it's not really feasible to pass with a full 13 HCP. You're therefore left with 1NT as the balancing action, which is right on points even though you don't have a full diamond stopper.

Okay, so if we can balance in notrump with these kinds of hands, how do we show the true 1NT overcall? Here is a table of guidelines to illustrate the procedure for balanced hands where a takeout double or overcall is not feasible:

Point Count	Direct Seat Actions	After an Opening Bid and Two Passes
12-14	Pass	1NT
15-18	1NT	double, then bid 1NT
19-20	double, then bid NT	double, then *jump* in NT

THE REMAINING BALANCING SITUATIONS

They bid and raise a minor

This is also a fairly safe auction to come into. Responder has denied a major and has opted to support opener's minor rather than bid 1NT, so he has some distribution. This bodes well for your side having a major-suit fit that you can play at the two-level.

For example:

♠ A Q 3   ♡ 10 8 7 2   ◇ 9   ♣ K 7 5 4 3

LHO	Partner	RHO	You
		1◇	pass
2◇	pass	pass	?

Partner most likely has close to opening points but has 3-4 diamonds and therefore not enough support for all the other suits to make a takeout double over the raise. As your support for the major suits is reasonable enough and you don't really want to commit to the three-level in clubs, doubling in passout chair and letting partner choose the suit is the most flexible choice.

They bid and raise a major

These auctions have two variants:

LHO	Partner	RHO	You
		1♠	pass
2♠	pass	pass	?

Once more, they've subsided in a partscore and established an eight-card fit. The difference between this and the minor-suit raise auction is that balancing takes you to the three-level, so vulnerability is definitely a consideration on whether you take the plunge. Still, if you have the distribution to handle any suit partner bids, it's worth a shot, even on a modest hand like:

♠ 5   ♡ Q J 8 4   ◇ A Q 9 2   ♣ 10 7 6 3

Since they haven't even tried for game, partner rates to have 10-13 points. Your side almost certainly has an eight-card fit of its own, so you shouldn't go quietly, as both sides could easily be able to make a partscore contract.

LHO	Partner	RHO	You
1◇	pass	1♡	pass
2♡	pass	pass	?

Here it's opener instead of responder supporting a major suit. The scenario is much the same, however. Since RHO hasn't even tried for game, your side will have in the neighborhood of 18 to 22 combined points.

What would you do on this auction with these two hands?

♠J96 ♡74 ◇KJ83 ♣AJ95

♠QJ75 ♡93 ◇A842 ♣KJ10

The first hand contains only three spades and has a shaky diamond holding in front of the opening bidder's suit. While taking the plunge might work out, the odds are against it. The second hand has better support for the unbid major and has the pure ◇A, and the general texture of the hand is more appealing. It's worthy of a balancing double.

Opener rebids 1NT and it gets passed back to you

LHO	Partner	RHO	You
1◇	pass	1♠	pass
1NT	pass	pass	?

This is a situation that is rife with danger in terms of a balancing action. Unlike the raise auctions, the opponents have not established an eight-card fit here. If they don't have a playable trump suit, you might not have one either.

To double in passout chair in a non-fit auction, a balanced hand should have near-opening or better values and tolerance for any unbid majors as that is where partner will head if he can't leave in a double.

♠AJ94 ♡QJ7 ◇86 ♣KJ98

A double, while optimistic, could easily work out here. If partner bids hearts or clubs you might be able to scramble a fair number of tricks on a crossruff as he won't have many spades and you're relatively short in LHO's diamonds.

They stop in a major-suit opener's second suit after a 1NT response

Of all the balancing situations, this one is the most perilous. Why? Consider this auction:

LHO	Partner	RHO	You
1♠	pass	1NT	pass
2◇	pass	pass	?

The opponents don't have a spade fit as responder hasn't supported the suit or even taken a belated preference. Opener has shown an unbalanced hand so the breaks in the other two suits might not be too friendly.

This isn't to say you won't ever balance here, but the quality of the suits can't be skimped upon regardless of whether you're overcalling or making a takeout double at this point. Here are a couple of examples to illustrate:

♠ 4 2   ♡ A Q 10 6   ◇ A 7   ♣ Q 9 8 6 3

Your unbid suit holdings are adequate and you have a near-opener pointwise, so you can go ahead and double for takeout.

♠ Q 9 2   ♡ A 7 6 4   ◇ K 10   ♣ K 9 8 5

It's somewhat more dangerous to compete with this hand, with two glitches in particular. One is in the spade suit, where they're likely to score a ruff on defense as RHO has not raised. Also, your 'body' in the unbid suits is not as good as on the first hand, and if responder is loaded in hearts and clubs, it will be tragic news for your side.

QUIZ HANDS

1) Vulnerable against not, you hold:

♠ K 8 3   ♡ Q 7   ♢ A J 7 5 4   ♣ K 8 5

West	North	East	South
			1♢
pass	1♡	1♠	?

What is your rebid now that East has overcalled?

2) Now no one is vulnerable as you hold:

♠ J 9 8 2   ♡ 9 8   ♢ A 9 3 2   ♣ K J 5

You find yourself confronted with an auction that dies fairly quickly as it comes around to you:

West	North	East	South
1♡	pass	pass	?

Should you let opener have it for 1♡ or not?

3) Now both sides are vulnerable, and you have this respectable-looking assortment:

♠ 8   ♡ K Q 9 5   ♢ K 6   ♣ A J 9 7 5 4

After both opponents have bid, you have a 'sandwich' decision to make:

West	North	East	South
1♢	pass	1♠	?

What are your thoughts? And action?

4) With no one vulnerable, your hand isn't quite as awe-inspiring this time out:

♠ 10 9 7 4   ♡ A 6   ♢ 7 6 3   ♣ A 10 7 6

West	North	East	South
pass	1♢	dbl	?

With this balanced 8-count, what's your pleasure as responder?

QUIZ HAND ANSWERS

1) North-South vul.

♠K 8 3   ♡Q 7   ◇A J 7 5 4   ♣K 8 5

West	North	East	South
			1◇
pass	1♡	1♠	?

East's intervention has converted a forcing situation for South into an optional one. A pass by opener will no longer end the auction as responder now has a further 'at-bat' coming to him. Keeping that in mind, it's generally not advisable for a minimum balanced opener to bid again voluntarily. The two exceptions are that you can raise with support or rebid 1NT with a double stopper in their suit. This hand contains neither of those attributes, and South should therefore pass. The entire hand is:

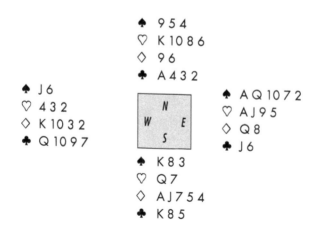

```
                    ♠  9 5 4
                    ♡  K 10 8 6
                    ◇  9 6
                    ♣  A 4 3 2
   ♠ J 6                              ♠ A Q 10 7 2
   ♡ 4 3 2          N                 ♡ A J 9 5
   ◇ K 10 3 2    W     E              ◇ Q 8
   ♣ Q 10 9 7        S                ♣ J 6
                    ♠  K 8 3
                    ♡  Q 7
                    ◇  A J 7 5 4
                    ♣  K 8 5
```

A pass will conclude the bidding as partner is at the low end of his response, but that is North-South's best result. Their 1♠ will either make or be a trick short, while either 1NT or 2◇ by your side is down a couple for an ugly -200.

2) Neither vul.

♠ J 9 8 2 ♡ 9 8 ◇ A 9 3 2 ♣ K J 5

West	North	East	South
1♡	pass	pass	?

Yes, it's only 9 HCP, but you should reopen with a takeout double. The auctions where an opening one-bid gets passed around to you are the safest ones in which to make an entrance, and you should do so with the appropriate distribution. Your hand has four spades and adequate holdings for the minors, so it's barely enough to try and give the opponents a jostle and not sell out. As it turns out, after a humdrum start, the rest of the auction gets fairly lively:

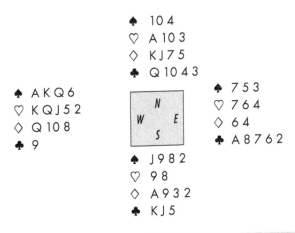

```
            ♠ 10 4
            ♡ A 10 3
            ◇ K J 7 5
            ♣ Q 10 4 3
♠ A K Q 6          N          ♠ 7 5 3
♡ K Q J 5 2    W       E      ♡ 7 6 4
◇ Q 10 8           S          ◇ 6 4
♣ 9                           ♣ A 8 7 6 2
            ♠ J 9 8 2
            ♡ 9 8
            ◇ A 9 3 2
            ♣ K J 5
```

West	North	East	South
1♡	pass	pass	dbl
1♠	2◇	2♡	pass
pass	3♣	pass	3◇
3♡	all pass		

After the balancing double, opener has enough to compete to the two-level and shows his other suit, spades, while he can do so conveniently.

North is thinking ahead when he bids 2◇, as he knows that East-West have an eight-card heart fit and will likely compete to 2♡. The odds favor having an adequate fit in one of the minors, but not necessarily both. In yet another example of the 'two bids or one' principle, he therefore lays the groundwork for arriving at the proper spot by mentioning diamonds, the higher ranked suit, first. Now, when the opponents bid 2♡ as expected, he introduces the clubs and voila! His side will now play their eight-card fit without having to go past the three-level, as South corrects to 3♢.

As for who can make what, East-West have eight tricks in a heart contract, so your side has to compete further to achieve a decent score. Your 3♢ will make no matter what. Even if the defense negotiates an immediate club ruff, eventually trumps can be drawn in two rounds and the heart loser goes on the fourth club. Their 3♡ has chances, but if North starts with a low trump, it is doomed to failure.

3)   Both vul.

♠8 ♡KQ95 ♢K6 ♣AJ9754

West	North	East	South
1♢	pass	1♠	?

This hand is another excursion into 'two bids or one?' territory. With a five-loser hand, it's definitely worth two actions if need be. But what should your first salvo be? It might seem natural to overcall the six-card suit, but you fully expect opener to be raising spades and now it will be a problem getting the heart suit in. Just as North did in the previous hand, you want to advertise both suits and enable the partnership to declare its best fit without having to risk the four-level. The first order of business, then, is to show the unbid suits with a takeout double. If partner shows no signs of life, you can introduce the clubs next time around and then he can make his choice, having a pretty fair idea of what your hand is.

The landscape of this deal happens to be:

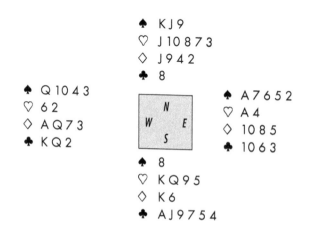

```
              ♠ K J 9
              ♡ J 10 8 7 3
              ◇ J 9 4 2
              ♣ 8
  ♠ Q 10 4 3         ┌─────┐      ♠ A 7 6 5 2
  ♡ 6 2              │  N  │      ♡ A 4
  ◇ A Q 7 3        W │     │ E    ◇ 10 8 5
  ♣ K Q 2           │  S  │      ♣ 10 6 3
                    └─────┘
              ♠ 8
              ♡ K Q 9 5
              ◇ K 6
              ♣ A J 9 7 5 4
```

When this hand was actually played, South overcalled 2♣ and found himself in a dither after opener raised to 2♠. He repeated the clubs (double would have still been a better choice) and went down two in 3♣ for an unpleasant result, losing two clubs, two diamonds and the two major-suit aces.

Suggested auction:

West	North	East	South
1◊	pass	1♠	dbl
2♠	pass	pass	3♣
pass	3♡	all pass	

Once South doubles to show the other two suits and then bids clubs, North has an easy correction to 3♡, knowing there is a nine-card fit there. North-South can make 3♡, while East-West will go down a trick if they persevere with 3♠.

Couldn't South have overcalled 2♣ and then bid 3♡ afterwards? Well, yes, and it would have turned out nicely on this particular hand, but I'm going to use my creative control to give two of North's hearts away, getting West's third club and one of East's spades in return. Now partner's hand becomes:

♠KJ95 ♡1073 ◊J942 ♣82

It won't be a fun hand for North-South regardless, but the 6-2 fit goes down least, as partner wouldn't have anything to say over 3♣ in the suggested auction. If the South hand bids clubs and hearts in that order, North's choice is between leaving overcaller in 3♡ or going back to 4♣ on his small doubleton.

Hands like this are very instructive, as they show the importance of:

- deciding if your cards are worth one or two actions, and...
- structuring those bids so as to give you enough of a safety margin in any competitive auction.

One final comment on the quiz hand is that while the loser count was five, this might be an optimistic evaluation considering the location of your ◊Kx, which is underneath the 1◊ opener. However, even if it turns out to be six losers instead of five, your cards, and more importantly your distribution, are sufficient to go into battle with the idea of taking two bids.

4)   Neither vul.

♠ 10 9 7 4   ♡ A 6   ◇ 7 6 3   ♣ A 10 7 6

West	North	East	South
pass	1◇	dbl	?

With two aces, you have enough to respond over the takeout double. Bidding 1♠ may seem repulsive, but it's forcing and you aren't going to be stranded there. If opener continues with 1NT, 2♣ or 2◇, you'll be perfectly all right. So why bother with that cruddy suit of yours, especially when RHO is showing spades with his double? Well, the 1♠ bid can still pay off, as I'll now unveil the hands of all the players:

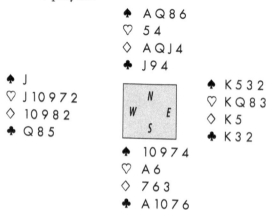

```
                    ♠ A Q 8 6
                    ♡ 5 4
                    ◇ A Q J 4
                    ♣ J 9 4
  ♠ J                              ♠ K 5 3 2
  ♡ J 10 9 7 2         N          ♡ K Q 8 3
  ◇ 10 9 8 2       W       E       ◇ K 5
  ♣ Q 8 5              S           ♣ K 3 2
                    ♠ 10 9 7 4
                    ♡ A 6
                    ◇ 7 6 3
                    ♣ A 10 7 6
```

Lo and behold, opener can raise your spades. The final contract is 2♠, making at least eight tricks and having decent chances for a ninth. If the final contract is 1NT, a heart lead will limit declarer to seven tricks.

CHAPTER 5

Notrump Auctions

In this chapter we're going to look at auctions that begin with an opening 1NT. First, we'll explore three popular conventions that allow your side to get into the auction over their notrump opening: Landy, Cappelletti, and DONT. Then we'll look at how you can deal with the situation after your side opens 1NT and the opponents overcall. I'm going to introduce the concept of the Lebensohl relay in these auctions, and show you how it can solve most of the new problems created by the interference. I'll also discuss some of the issues that come up when you've doubled their 1NT opening for penalties.

What to Play over Their 1NT Opening?

The landscape for competing against a 1NT opening has changed in two respects over the years. The first is that it's no longer a given that a notrump opener will be 15-17, and you will come across a fair number of partnerships using a lower range. A weak notrump opener is typically about a king less on both the low and high end, the most common variations being 12-14, 12-15 and 13-15. Along with the general trend toward competing more aggressively, this development has led to an increased frequency of bidding over an enemy 1NT and the invention of an abundance of ways to do so.

In fact, the opponents' notrump range should have little effect on what assets you need to compete in direct seat. For obvious reasons, you should abide by the same principles that apply to any two-level overcall. Points are nice, but strong distributional features are even more essential.

About three years ago after a club game, a friend wanted to discuss one hand in particular with me, as we had been playing in the same direction. His RHO opened a 15-17 point 1NT and he held:

♠ K Q 10 7 6   ♡ J 9 5   ◇ A 7   ♣ K J 4

He duly overcalled 2♠. When the hand was played at my table I passed the 1NT opening, not out of innate brilliance but on account of having seen this kind of movie before. This was partner's hand:

♠ J 5 3   ♡ 10 6 3 2   ◇ K J 9   ♣ 7 6 4

My friend went down in 2♠, and the sadness was that 1NT would have failed by two tricks on the normal lead of the ♠K.

Here is what can be learned from results like this:

- Some hands are not as good as the point count would suggest, and this was one of them. The ♡J does not rate to be worth much. As for the ♣KJx, you'll need to lead up to them twice to convert them into tricks, and you probably won't have the entries to manage it. The high-card points are 14, but I'd discount one or both of the jacks.
- With 15-17 on your right and 14 in your own hand, that only leaves 9-11 between LHO and partner. In view of that, the dummy that greeted my friend was about what he could expect. It also contained three-card spade support plus the working ◇K, but that still wasn't enough.
- Let's consider how the distribution of the missing 9-11 HCP will affect the outcome of the deal:
  - » If LHO has most of it, the news is bad. You'll go down two or three and might even get doubled.
  - » If partner has most of it, you'll make 2♠ but the news is still bad. Why? You have a better score available from defending 1NT and holding it to three or four tricks.
  - » If partner has some of it, you'll have a mixed bag of results. Much of it depends on the vulnerability and how well they'd have done in 1NT.

To wrap up the analysis, venturing in over their 1NT on a balanced 11-14 is a chancy proposition. It helps considerably if you have a more distributional hand.

A couple of weeks later, I ran into a situation in which the direct-seat player had a vastly different hand when RHO opened 1NT:

♠AQ974 ♡A9632 ◇853 ♣—

With 5-5 shape, the player with these cards overcalled 2♠, the higher-ranking of his suits. This time at least he managed to go plus, as partner had:

♠108 ♡J10975 ◇6 ♣AJ743

His side could make nine tricks in spades, while 1NT their way has fair chances on anything but a heart lead. The downer, though, was that they missed the 5-5 fit in hearts that could produce eleven tricks. It would have been nice to have a way to show both majors, but to accomplish that you have to give up a natural bid. Which one should it be?

In this chapter, we're going to look at three popular ways of competing against a 1NT opening, and if you do some research you will find that there are many, many more (two others are discussed in Chapter 9). Most of them toss the natural 2♣ bid overboard in favor of some artificial usage. There's a logical reason for that choice, as a natural overcall of the lowest-ranking suit will seldom buy the contract. Either responder or perhaps even the 1NT opener will contest the auction further.

The Simple Option — Landy

Landy, the first of the conventions I'll describe, is not the most popular — Cappelletti and DONT, which we'll look at next, both have greater followings. It is, however, the simplest because all the bids mean precisely what they say with the exception of 2♣. The 2♣ overcall becomes your mechanism for showing both majors. Overcaller should have at least nine and preferably ten major-suit cards. That bid would have been a godsend on the last hand, where the overcalling side would have quickly arrived in a heart contract, perhaps even at the game level.

Suppose partner has unleashed his Landy 2♣ bid on you:

LHO	Partner	RHO	You
1NT	2♣*	pass	?

and you're looking at:

♠ J 4   ♡ 10 6   ◇ A Q 10 5   ♣ 9 7 6 4 3

Hmmm, looks as if you'll have to pick a major, but which one? You could just bid 2♡ and hope it's the right choice. What if partner has four spades and five hearts, though? One option, provided you discuss it with partner beforehand, is to use a bid of 2◇ now as showing no marked preference between the majors and asking the overcaller to choose the suit he's longer and/or stronger in.

With Landy now in place, let's look at some hands and decide whether they justify taking action over a 1NT opening:

♠ A 9 8 6 5   ♡ K Q J 9   ◇ A 2   ♣ 7 5

This hand is borderline, but you have a sound opener plus a mildly unbalanced hand. If you do elect to bid, the best option is 2♣, to show the majors, since a 2♠ overcall could miss a better fit in the heart suit. Whichever of your two suits partner chooses, you should get to a playable contract.

♠ Q J 6   ♡ 10   ◇ K 10 9 7 4 2   ♣ A Q 7

Overcall 2◇. A 'mere' 12-count, but the losing trick count is six, and with an unbalanced hand, there should be no qualms about overcalling.

♠ K J 4   ♡ K 8 7 6 2   ◇ A 10 8   ♣ Q 9

Not this time: eight losers, a balanced hand, and uninspiring quality in the long suit. Pass and lead hearts. If partner has enough for you to make 2♡, you should be able to ravage 1NT on defense.

♠ A Q 8   ♡ K 10 6   ◇ A Q J 9 7   ♣ 6 3

Double. With a standout lead in the ◇Q, you should be well positioned to defeat their contract if partner has even one trick in his hand.

Landy is a reasonable starting point for competing against a 1NT opening, particularly if your bridge experience is limited. I'd suggest trying it for a few months. At that point, you could be quite satisfied with your results and not have any inclination to change. Alternatively, you might want to try something that enables you to get into the bidding on a greater variety of hands. If so, there are plenty of other methods to choose from.

The Popular Option — Cappelletti

Although the numbers may have leveled off recently, in the past twenty years there has been a significant departure from the strong 1NT opening in favor of the weak notrump. That being the case, many players like to be able to have a penalty double available for dealing with the lesser-strength versions of the notrump opening.

Landy retains the penalty double, to be sure, but the only two-suited hand it can show is the majors. Mike Cappelletti developed a convention (also known as Hamilton or Pottage — the exact name for this convention tends to be a matter of regional preference, since several people came up with the idea at about the same time) that retained the penalty double and enabled the user to show a variety of two-suited hands. He accomplished this by using the cheapest bid, 2♣, as an artificial way to announce an unspecified one-suited hand, and the remaining two-level bids to show the various two-suiters.

Here are the bids and their meanings in the Cappelletti scheme of things:

Double   Penalty.

The first order of business is to set the range for a penalty double, because there is actually a divergence of opinion on what is required. Some pairs allow the double on a hand equivalent to the opponents' notrump range. As a starting point, I would suggest that a penalty double meet these two criteria, whatever kind of notrump you are doubling:

- 15 or more HCP.
- You should be certain of what your opening lead is going to be, rather than 'going into the tank' and agonizing about it.

Here are three hands to think about and decide whether they justify a penalty double of a weak (12-14) 1NT:

♠A3 ♡KQ96 ♢AJ4 ♣QJ98

♠A102 ♡KQ9 ♢A654 ♣Q104

♠AK6 ♡107 ♢QJ1085 ♣AJ10

Do you have the answer? The first hand, with 17 HCP and two plausible leads in hearts and clubs, is worth a double. The third hand is also worth a double, even with only 15 points, since the ♢Q is a standout lead that will eventually produce tricks in that suit. The second hand, also 15 HCP, has no appealing lead. Any of the four suits could be right... or wrong. With that hand you should pass and not commit to a penalty double, as you could easily be wrong in assuming the hand belongs to your side.

2♣   *Any* one-suited hand. Asks partner to bid 2♢, after which you'll then reveal your suit.

2♢   The majors. You should be 5-5 in hearts and spades. If your side is not vulnerable or in balancing seat, you might chance it on 5-4 if the four-card suit is very good. You'd venture in with 2♢ on:

♠QJ872 ♡AQ1065 ♢84 ♣7

Even with a mere 9 points, this hand is unbalanced with two decent five-card suits, and you shouldn't shy away from bidding.

♠A K J 5   ♡Q 10 7 6 2   ◇9 6   ♣A 4

This hand isn't quite as shapely, but has additional high-card strength. While you don't have 5-5 in the majors, with the robust spade holding, it certainly *feels* like a two-suiter, so again 2◇ would be perfectly acceptable.

♠Q 7 4 2   ♡A K J 10 6   ◇K 9   ♣6 5

On this hand, use the artificial 2♣ instead, and then correct to hearts over partner's forced 2◇. The quality and length of the spades pale in comparison to the hearts, so treat this hand as a one-suiter.

2♡	Hearts and a minor. Here even more so than with the 2◇ bid, the minor should be five cards long as you're going to be playing at the three-level if partner doesn't care for your hearts. To escape to your minor, partner bids 2NT to inquire as to what suit it is, whereupon you'll answer with 3♣ or 3◇.
2♠	Spades and a minor. Again, partner can ask for the minor with 2NT.
2NT	The minor suits, 5-5 or better.
3♣/3◇	A jump to three of a minor is typically preemptive with a long suit. With a stronger hand, you'd begin with a penalty double or 2♣.
3♡/3♠	The meaning of a jump to three of a major is something every partnership should discuss. Natural and preemptive would be one of the two choices. The alternative would be to play it as showing a distributional hand with game interest, along the lines of:

♠8   ♡A K J 9 8 5 2   ◇A Q J   ♣7 3

To conclude this section, here's an example of how the one-suited hand would be shown in Cappelletti, as you pick up:

♠ K Q 10 9 6   ♡ 10 6   ◇ A 5   ♣ A 8 4 3

LHO	Partner	RHO	You
		1NT	2♣*
pass	2◇*	pass	2♠
all pass			

Granted, you do have clubs as well as spades, but they aren't particularly good and the wonderful spades are the primary feature of the hand. That's why it should be treated as a one-suiter.

The above hand is similar to one from earlier in the chapter, where I suggested passing rather than bidding. However, there are two aspects to this one that make a fair amount of difference. First, your outside values here are sure tricks in the form of aces. Furthermore, the 5422 distribution is a mild upgrade from 5332 that reduces the losing trick count to six.

Giving partner the same nondescript five-count as before, we now have:

Dummy   ♠ J 7 2   ♡ J 7 5 4   ◇ K J 9   ♣ 7 6 2

You   ♠ K Q 10 9 6   ♡ 10 6   ◇ A 5   ♣ A 8 4 3

Now your 2♠ contract will come home with eight tricks more often than not, while 1NT will only go down two at most. If you recall the chart of distribution types from the start of the book, I said that the further right you move towards the more unbalanced hand patterns, the safer it is to bid in competition. This is yet another illustration of that principle.

The Aggressive Option — DONT

From the time Cappelletti was introduced in the 1970s, there was a lull of close to twenty years where no fresh ideas of competing against 1NT openings emerged as popular alternatives. However, there was a growing uncertainty about whether any one convention was the perfect answer against all notrump ranges. There are three things you'd potentially like to be able to do when they open 1NT. They are:

- double them for penalties.
- show unbalanced one-suiters.
- show unbalanced two-suiters.

Unfortunately, it's difficult to cram all of these hand types into a relatively limited amount of bidding space. So which of them are the most important?

Against a weak notrump, many players are fond of Cappelletti because they like to have the penalty double available. In addition, the one-suited hand (except for clubs) and the major two-suiter can be described without having to venture higher than you'd want to. You can show the other two-suiters as well, although you might have to go to the three-level to play in your best fit.

When you're up against a strong notrump, hands that are worth a penalty double are not as frequent because there are more points that are already spoken for by the opening bidder. That aspect of competing is no longer the main priority for your side. Conversely, you'd like to advertise the two-suited hands without going past the two-level as you are sometimes forced to do in Cappelletti.

In the September/October 1989 issue of *Bridge Today* magazine, Marty Bergen and Larry Cohen proposed a new convention for bidding against a 1NT opening. It quickly found a willing audience and prompted other theorists to devise treatments for competing over the enemy 1NT, a process that continues in full swing to this day.

The Bergen-Cohen brainchild is known as DONT, an acronym for Disturbing Opponents' NoTrump. In a nutshell, DONT sacrifices the penalty double in return for the ability to stay at the two-level any time you compete with a one- or two-suited hand.

Here are the particulars of DONT when the opponents open 1NT:

Double	Shows any one-suited hand, and asks partner to bid 2♣. The doubler then passes if he has clubs and otherwise bids his long suit.
Two-level bids	With the exception of 2♠, these actions show two-suited hands, the bid suit along with a higher-ranked one. Looking at each of them in turn, we have:
2♣	Clubs and one of the other three suits.
2◇	Diamonds and a major
2♡	Specifically hearts and spades, as that is the only higher-ranking suit.
2♠	There is no suit higher-ranking than spades, so this bid must therefore be a natural one-suiter.

As a result, in the DONT structure, you now have two ways of ways of showing spades — you can bid 2♠ directly, or double and then bid 2♠. Is there a difference between these auctions?

Yes, there is. The first sequence takes away a lot of their bidding room, while the second one doesn't. Consequently, the immediate 2♠ is more destructive in nature, and the bid is typically anywhere from a respectable weak-two to a marginal opening bid. To double and *then* bid 2♠, the slower approach, shows possession of at least sound opening values.

With the DONT framework in place, let's look at some example hands:

LHO	Partner	RHO	You
		1NT	?

♠86 ♡KJ6 ◇AQJ10 7 5 ♣J3

Double, to show a one-suited hand. You're asking partner to bid 2♣, over which you'll reveal your suit with 2◇.

♠K 10 8 4 3 ♡K 5 ◇AQ872 ♣6

Bid 2◇, promising diamonds and a higher suit. By contrast, using Landy, you'd have no way to describe this major-minor hand. Playing Cappelletti, you can bid 2♠ to show that suit and a minor, but if partner doesn't like spades, you'll have to go one level higher to play in diamonds. In the DONT scheme of things, you can remain at the two-level while locating an adequate fit.

♠QJ10 9 6 4 ♡3 ◇AJ7 ♣10 5 2

Bid 2♠. The 'mini' 2♠ overcall, on a hand with a long suit but not bursting at the seams with high-card points. Partner will know that the fast way of getting to 2♠ shows little interest in game.

♠KJ10 7 6 4 ♡9 4 ◇K3 ♣AQ5

Double, followed by 2♠ when partner bids the requested 2♣. Taking the meandering route to show the spades confirms full opening points and every intention of buying the contract.

What about the partner of the DONT bidder? What role does he play? Let's travel across the table and look at things from that perspective.

LHO	Partner	RHO	You
1NT	dbl	pass	?

♠ Q 8 6 5 4 2　♡ A 9　♢ 7 6 5　♣ 8 6

Bid 2♣, following partner's instructions so that he can show his suit. Yes, you have a long suit of your own, but partner's could be better. There is no pressing reason to suggest another direction with this hand.

♠ 9 6 2　♡ K Q 10 8 7 4　♢ Q 3 2　♣ 7

Bid 2♡. This is a different situation, as you'd like to place a strong vote for hearts being the trumps suit for your side. Partner's suit may well be clubs, and you may well have a better fit in hearts.

LHO	Partner	RHO	You
1NT	2◇*	pass	?

♠ J 6　♡ Q 4　♢ K 9 7 2　♣ 10 8 6 5 3

Pass. No problem here. Partner has struck gold with his 2◇, showing diamonds and a major. You have a good fit and no desire to play his other suit.

♠ 10 7 6 5　♡ Q 8 2　♢ 9 4　♣ K 7 4 2

Bid 2♡. Partner's major will be a better spot for you than diamonds. He'll now pass or convert to 2♠, depending on what his other suit is.

♠ 6 3　♡ Q 8 7 5　♢ J 6　♣ K 10 7 5 4

Pass. Yes, you might have a heart fit, but only if that is partner's other suit, and it's equally or more likely that his major is spades. If you try a hopeful 2♡ and he now continues with 2♠, you'd like to retract your bid and go back to 2◇, but they probably won't let you.

A key element of DONT is that when partner makes a two-suited bid and you want to play in the other one, you should:

- be well prepared for whatever that suit is
- remember that the drill is to make the cheapest bid in these instances, in case that is partner's other suit.

With the second example hand you're willing to play hearts *or* spades, and can bid 2♡ to head for overcaller's major. With the third hand you can't handle partner's major being spades and so you are best off passing 2♢, which is going to be at least a 5-2 fit.

Decisions, Decisions

We've had a look at three methods of competing against the opponents' 1NT opening but there are scads more — in fact, I'll discuss two more in Chapter 9. If you're sufficiently curious to have a look at the whole bunch, David Stevenson has a website that lists 108 defenses to a 1NT opening.

As you browse through this variety of systems, there are several things to keep in mind. All of them have to give up *something*. For example, having the penalty double and natural major-suit overcalls restricts the ability to show two-suited hands. Conversely, a treatment such as DONT will permit you to describe all two-suited hands and play at the cheapest level, but you give up the penalty double and the one-suiters are shown in a roundabout fashion. The bottom line is that there isn't enough space to have it all, so you have to choose what is most essential in your opinion. It's a matter of you and partner getting together to determine what your main priorities are. Then you can select a defense that meets your needs and just as importantly, won't be forgotten in the heat of battle. If you prefer a convention that requires little memory work, Landy fits the bill as there is only one artificial bid, 2♣ to show the majors. Frankly, though, it's somewhat limited as to the number of hand patterns you can show. That's why Cappelletti and DONT are more frequently chosen.

The other issue is deciding whether or not to have one system against weak notrumps and another against strong. Some players insist that you have to vary your methods of getting into the fray according to their notrump range. They want to have penalty doubles in their bag against lesser notrumps but more and safer ways of bidding versus the 15-17 1NT. Perhaps that's the optimum approach, but you and partner shouldn't feel obligated to go with that flow if you aren't entirely convinced of it — and it certainly involves more memory work. Many pairs do just fine using one defense for all ranges.

The Penalty Double and its Continuations

Suppose you and partner have a defense to 1NT that includes a penalty double. If you leave the discussion at that without going into further detail, you're liable to experience some headaches as the auction moves along. You should clarify and nail down five key aspects of the process:

1) How good a hand is required for the double?

I talked about this somewhat earlier in this chapter. Some are fairly stringent and prefer that the doubler have at least 15 or 16 HCP and an attractive lead. There are also proponents of 'equal or better', so that if their 1NT is 12-14, then the doubler might have as few as 12 HCP, although he could be much stronger. Others still would compromise in the middle at 14+ HCP. My own opinion is that hands of 11 to a bad 14 can bid with shape, but should pass if balanced, so the double would require something more.

2) How about doubles in passout chair?

They can be scaled down a tad and be anywhere from a decent 11 HCP upwards.

3) With what type of hand should you remove the double?

If you are weaker than 6 HCP and have unbalanced distribution, you might consider pulling. Otherwise, you're best off standing your ground. How do you go about reaching your destination? Some players expect the bidding will be natural, while others treat the auction as if the doubler had opened 1NT and presume that systems are on. You'll want to talk to partner and get his input so that you don't have auctions like these going off the rails.

4) What should your side do if the opponents run out from a penalty double of their 1NT?

Are they allowed to play their contract undoubled or is your side committed either to whack it or bid on? If they are weak notrumpers, many partnerships agree that the opener's side is not allowed to play undoubled below 2♠, but this whole area must be discussed thoroughly. Your decisions may impact the answer to the next question.

5) Are later doubles takeout or business?

LHO	Partner	RHO	You
		1NT	dbl
2♡	dbl		

LHO is showing 5+ hearts and a poor hand. Using this sequence as an example, what is your interpretation of partner's double?

Well, of course the double is penalty, you might say. That is certainly reasonable, and is how we operate in my partnerships because the double is what it sounds like, that they're going down.

However, some pairs use the opposite tactic and apply negative double principles to this situation. With that agreement, partner's double would promise 7+ HCP and shortness in the enemy suit. You will then either bid or, if you have heart length, convert the double for penalties. If partner instead passes in direct seat, he'll have either points with hearts or an awful hand. You then reopen with a double (or bid) any time you have two or fewer in their suit.

I have no strong feelings on whether to use penalty or takeout doubles in direct seat once they've made their escape from 1NT. Both schools of thought have numerous adherents, because it's a virtual tossup on which of the two approaches is superior. As always, the most important thing is to have an agreement.

When They Interfere with Your 1NT: Prelude

Having looked at ways to get in when the opponents open 1NT, let's discuss what happens when they are unkind enough to interfere in your notrump auctions. Nowadays the opponents are more apt to butt in over your side's 1NT, even when the range is 15-17 HCP. Maybe, as responder, your hand will be such that their interference isn't particularly bothersome, but at times you're left in a ticklish situation for a couple of reasons. One is that you might have no bid that really stands out. The other is that you and partner might not be on the same wavelength as to what bids are forcing, invitational or merely competitive.

Here is a fair sampling of the hand types that might occur when partner opens 1NT and they intrude in the bidding:

LHO	Partner	RHO	You
	1NT	2♡	?

♠ Q 7 4   ♡ 6 5   ◇ 8 3   ♣ K 10 8 7 5 2

What are your inclinations with this hand? Your side has at least half the points in the deck and a playable club fit is guaranteed since opener has two or more of them. It makes sense to compete to 3♣, then, but you don't want partner to get excited and bid game.

♠ J 6   ♡ 7 5   ◇ K 10   ♣ K J 9 6 5 3 2

Once more, you'd like to have the security of being in your long suit if this is a partscore hand. The glitch here, though, is if partner has a maximum 1NT opening with heart stopper(s), you could be missing game, especially if he has a club card. You'd like to be able to show invitational rather than competitive values without having to go past the most likely game contract of 3NT.

♠ Q 9 6 ♡ K 2 ♢ A J 10 8 5 ♣ J 7 4

No problem here. You have the values for game and a high card in the suit they've bid, so bidding 3NT looks right.

♠ Q 9 6 ♡ 6 5 ♢ A J 10 8 5 ♣ K J 4

Same point-count, but with the notable difference that you lack a heart stopper. How can you be certain that the opponents won't run the suit? It would be a shame to bypass 3NT only to discover that opener had sufficient protection against a heart lead.

Tinkering with the auction a bit, we'll now switch over to:

LHO	Partner	RHO	You
	1NT	2♠	?

♠ 10 6 ♡ K 9 5 4 3 ♢ A 8 6 ♣ A 10 7

Your side belongs in game, but where? If partner has only two hearts, 4♡ might be an unhappy contract. But 3NT isn't very attractive with your small doubleton in spades, and you might have an eight-card fit in your long suit. How can you find out for sure?

♠ 9 5 ♡ Q J 8 6 4 ♢ A J 10 ♣ 6 5 2

Here again you have a five-card major together with 8 HCP, worth an invite but not necessarily enough for game. With not much bidding space left, how can you describe *this* hand?

♠ J 3 ♡ A 10 5 4 ♢ K J 9 ♣ Q 8 5 2

Houston, there is a definite problem here! This hand was supposed to be a total breeze to bid: start with Stayman to find out if opener has hearts, and then park the contract in 4♡ or 3NT. But those infernal opponents went and crashed the party with their 2♠ bid. You still intend to reach game, but how do you check for a possible heart fit now, not to mention finding out whether your side has spades stopped?

The Solution: SSS and Lebensohl

Fortunately, all of the preceding challenges can be deftly handled through the use of a couple of techniques. They are:

- Same-Suit Stayman (or SSS for short)
- Lebensohl

The first step towards dealing with their overcall is to ask for majors via a cuebid of the enemy suit. Ergo, in this auction:

LHO	Partner	RHO	You
	1NT	2♠	3♠

the 3♠ bid is Stayman, asking opener if he has 4+ hearts. There is, however, a crucial difference from 'normal' Stayman to keep in mind. In a free-run auction, Stayman can be used with invitational or better hands. Once the bidding turns competitive, responder needs game-forcing values to trot out same-suit Stayman, as there is no longer room to invite.

The other linchpin for handling the opponents' interference is to convert 2NT by responder into an artificial bid, which simply asks opener to bid 3♣ — a convention called Lebensohl.

What is the idea behind the 2NT relay? Well, before we get to that, let's define what the immediate three-level bids mean. There are four of them:

- Three of a minor: invitational, five-card or longer suit.
- Three of a major: natural and game-forcing.
- Three of their suit: same-suit Stayman, looking for a 4-4 major suit fit.
- 3NT: values for game, no major-suit length.

There are two main objectives in using Lebensohl. The first is to allow responder to vie for the contract without overstating the quality of his hand. The second is to clarify whether responder has the opponents' suit stopped when there are enough points for game. You may have heard the expression 'slow shows, fast denies' applied to Lebensohl auctions. That means that an *immediate* same-suit Stayman or 3NT denies any tangible help in staving off the run of their suit. If you precede those bids with the 2NT relay, you're showing a high card in their suit.

Having developed those themes, we can move on to the precise intent of the 2NT bid, which is to allow you to do the following:

- to compete in an unbid minor without inviting game.
- to invite game in an unbid major.

- to show game values *and* promise a stopper in their suit.

Are there any hands that responder can't adequately describe in the Lebensohl structure? Yes, if he has a balanced 8-9 HCP with no five-card suit, he is stuck because 2NT is now a conventional rather than a natural bid. With those hands, the options will be to pass, double for penalties, or bid a reasonable four-card suit at the two-level in the hope that opener will have three or more of them. In the meantime, the gains from Lebensohl will far outweigh the minor inconvenience of losing the original meaning of a 2NT response.

The proof is in the pudding, as they say, so let's see some hands that will both familiarize you with and let you appreciate the value of Lebensohl.

LHO	Partner	RHO	You
	1NT	2♠	?

♠7 ♡J93 ◇Q76542 ♣K85

Bid 2NT, asking opener to bid 3♣. You'll then correct to 3◇, which is to play and shows no game interest. The long diamonds and shortness in their suit are enough to try and buy the contract at the three-level, despite the meager point-count.

♠64 ♡A72 ◇J85 ♣KJ962

Bid 3♣. Here, you do have some game interest, but not quite enough to make that commitment. For 3NT to have a play, opener will need both a high card in clubs and their suit adequately stopped. By bidding a direct 3♣, rather than getting there via the Lebensohl 2NT, you convey the message of a long suit and an invitational hand. To see how nicely this framework operates, take a look at what partner has for his 1NT opening and match the examples with it:

Partner

♠AJ87 ♡KQ84 ◇A10 ♣Q103

With the first of the responder hands, you'll end up playing 3◇, but opposite the second hand where you invite with 3♣, opener will bid 3NT with his good fillers in clubs and a double spade stopper.

Are you ready now for a dose of the 'slow shows, fast denies' principle? Here we go...

LHO	Partner	RHO	You
	1NT	2♠	?

♠954 ♡1042 ◇KQJ98 ♣A7

Bid an immediate 3NT, telling opener you have the values for game but no help insofar as spade stoppers are concerned.

♠A107 ♡763 ◇KQJ94 ♣105

This time you bid 2NT, relaying to 3♣, and continue with a delayed 3NT. In this manner you'll confirm a high card in their suit, which may ease partner's fears about a spade lead.

Here's opener's hand:

Partner

♠J3 ♡KQ85 ◇A106 ♣KQJ9

On the 'slow' second auction where you promise a spade stopper, opener will pass and 3NT will make in comfort. Your ♠10 is a bonus as it now gives your side a likely double stopper.

After the straight blast to 3NT with the first example hand, opener will remove to 4♣ since you've indicated no help in spades and he can't stop them from running the suit. Your side will wind up in 4◇ after you correct to your long minor.

Sometimes their interference will leave you a few more options. What are bids in a new suit at the two-level by responder, if they are available?

LHO	Partner	RHO	You
	1NT	2♡	?

Bidding 2♠ here should be a natural signoff, with no game interest.

You'll note from the above that despite the fancy name, most bids in the Lebensohl environment are natural. Even the 2NT relay is a lead-in to a further descriptive action by responder. It's therefore incompatible with keeping your usual system (e.g. transfers) on when the opponents compete over your 1NT. You have to decide between one and the other. However, in Chapter 8 I'll elaborate more on situations where you might logically want to retain a 'systems on' approach in competition.

1) You're vulnerable, and you hold:

♠ K 10 8 7 6 5   ♡ K 7   ◇ 3   ♣ A J 10 8

the bidding has commenced with:

West	North	East	South
	pass	1NT	?

First off, is this hand good enough to compete?
If you think it is, what should your action be playing:

a) Landy?
b) Cappelletti?
c) DONT?

2) They're vulnerable and you're not, as you're dealt these cards:

♠ K Q 10 4   ♡ 10 9   ◇ K J 10 8 7   ♣ 5 2

The auction has ground to a halt with:

West	North	East	South
1NT	pass	pass	?

Should this hand go quietly or not?

3) You're vulnerable against not, but at least you get some attractive distribution for this one:

♠ A Q 7 6 5   ♡ 9 5   ◇ 10   ♣ Q 10 7 6 5

Needless to say, they barge right in after partner opens:

West	North	East	South
	1NT	2♡	?

Assume that you're playing Lebensohl. Do you remember the way to show this kind of hand?

4) Neither side vulnerable and your share of the cards is very meager:

♠ 8 4   ♡ 9 6 5 3 2   ◇ K 10 5 4   ♣ Q 8

It turns out an important decision falls on your shoulders as the auction goes

West	North	East	South
1NT*	dbl	pass	?

LHO's 1NT opening shows 12-14 HCP, and partner's double is for penalty. Do you leave it in or not?

1)   North-South vul.

♠ K 10 8 7 6 5 ♡ K 7 ◇ 3 ♣ A J 10 8

West	North	East	South
	pass	1NT	?

As I've emphasized throughout the first two chapters, having an unbalanced hand is a must for bidding at the two-level once they have opened and especially if RHO has opened 1NT. With ten cards in the black suits, the hand contains enough shape to venture into the fray.

How best to show this hand in the various notrump defenses?

a) Landy — 2♠. No other choice, as the only two-suited hands you can show are the majors.

b) Cappelletti — 2♠, to show spades and a minor. If partner has a few of your spades, you'll be in a good spot. If he has a singleton, then he'll ask for your minor with 2NT and you'll play in 3♣.

c) DONT. While you do have 2♣ in your quiver to advertise clubs and a higher suit, this would not be the time to use it. Partner would leave you there with three of them (or perhaps even a doubleton honor), thereby possibly missing out on a better and higher paying destination in the spade suit. The odds are in your favor to go with the one-suited double and then continue with 2♠, hoping you'll be getting two or more of your long suit in dummy.

This is a good illustration of how system can affect your bid on a particular hand. In Cappelletti, it's convenient enough to show the two suits as you're bidding the longer one directly. In DONT, you don't have that luxury so it's best to treat the hand as a one-suiter.

The end result will be decent for your side, as witness:

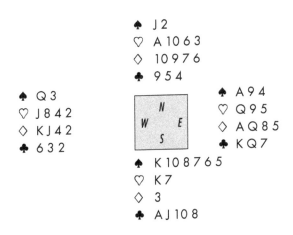

```
              ♠ J 2
              ♡ A 10 6 3
              ◇ 10 9 7 6
              ♣ 9 5 4
  ♠ Q 3                      ♠ A 9 4
  ♡ J 8 4 2         N        ♡ Q 9 5
  ◇ K J 4 2    W        E    ◇ A Q 8 5
  ♣ 6 3 2           S        ♣ K Q 7
              ♠ K 10 8 7 6 5
              ♡ K 7
              ◇ 3
              ♣ A J 10 8
```

Their 1NT can make if South leads a spade. Once again, both sides can make a partial as 2♠ will lose only a diamond, two trumps and one or two clubs. West has no appealing choices in a competitive auction, and your bid will likely buy the contract.

2)   East-West vul.

♠ K Q 10 4   ♡ 10 9   ◇ K J 10 8 7   ♣ 5 2

West	North	East	South
1NT	pass	pass	?

This one is by no means automatic, but with the colors in your favor, bidding is worth a shot here. Your hand is 'only' 9 HCP, but it's mildly unbalanced at 5422 shape, and the loser count is seven. A further plus is that the long suits contain all of your high cards and also have the 10-spots to bolster them. In DONT, you'd consider this to be a two-suited hand and bid 2◇ to show diamonds and a major.

How do you fare with this entry into the auction? You get a rather nice buy for dummy, as witness:

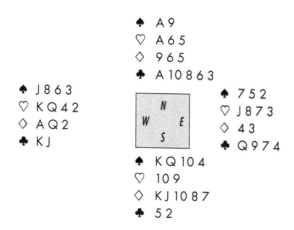

```
                    ♠ A 9
                    ♡ A 6 5
                    ◇ 9 6 5
                    ♣ A 10 8 6 3
  ♠ J 8 6 3                        ♠ 7 5 2
  ♡ K Q 4 2          N             ♡ J 8 7 3
  ◇ A Q 2        W       E         ◇ 4 3
  ♣ K J              S             ♣ Q 9 7 4
                    ♠ K Q 10 4
                    ♡ 10 9
                    ◇ K J 10 8 7
                    ♣ 5 2
```

North has more high-card points, but the shape is too balanced and the long suit not quite strong enough for him to act in direct seat. If he decides to venture a bid, the upshot will be a 2♣ contract with six total losers, an embarrassing three of them in the trump suit itself. However, 2◇ by South is a happier story, as declarer can hold his losers to four: two diamonds and a trick each in clubs and hearts.

While the overcaller here might have got more than he actually deserved, his bid still has a fair chance of producing a good result. Suppose we move the ♠A from North to East. Now 2◇ will probably go down, but South doesn't much care as his -50 or -100 is still better than the -120 he gives up by selling out to 1NT.

How would South act if his partnership's convention of choice is Cappelletti rather than DONT? Now he can't realistically bid 2♠ to show that suit and a minor with only four spades, so the options are to pass or bid the artificial 2♣ to show any one-suited hand. These last two examples are great illustrations of how no defensive method over 1NT is always an ideal fit. This one fits DONT like a glove, whereas the previous one was better for Cappelletti.

3)   North-South vul.

♠ A Q 7 6 5   ♡ 9 5   ◇ 10   ♣ Q 10 7 6 5

West	North	East	South
	1NT	2♡	?

With 5-5 shape and some points, you're assuredly in the mood to compete. Before introducing the spades, though, let's consider if you're interested in game.

Yes, although your 8 HCP aren't quite enough to go all the way, the hand is worth a game try. As mentioned earlier, there is a way to invite game in an unbid major in the Lebehsohl scheme of things.

Bidding 2♠ would be to play, with no game interest. A direct 3♠ shows 10+ points and most often precisely five spades. The way to show the in-between hand of 8-9 points is to use the artificial 2NT followed by 3♠ over partner's required 3♣. Opener will then place the contract, and in this case he bids 3NT. Not your preferred choice, perhaps, but he's denied three-card spade support so you might as well grit your teeth and pass.

Your trust in partner's decision-making ability will be rewarded as the complete layout of the hand is:

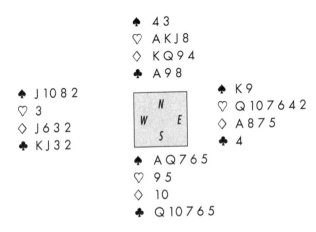

```
              ♠ 4 3
              ♡ A K J 8
              ◇ K Q 9 4
              ♣ A 9 8
♠ J 10 8 2              ♠ K 9
♡ 3            N        ♡ Q 10 7 6 4 2
◇ J 6 3 2    W   E      ◇ A 8 7 5
♣ K J 3 2      S        ♣ 4
              ♠ A Q 7 6 5
              ♡ 9 5
              ◇ 10
              ♣ Q 10 7 6 5
```

There's both good and bad news in 3NT. The spade finesse works but the suit divides 4-2. You may well lose two tricks in clubs. But East has no reason to lead anything but a heart, which gives declarer an extra trick, and the ◇J is onside, so the defense can't attack that suit profitably.

What should declarer's plan be? There are more combined spot cards in clubs, so he should go after that suit at the beginning. By working on clubs first and taking the spade finesse later, he will garner three club tricks, two spades and four or five tricks in the red suits, bringing home the contract.

4) Neither vul.

♠ 8 4   ♡ 9 6 5 3 2   ◇ K 10 5 4   ♣ Q 8

West	North	East	South
1NT[1]	dbl	pass	?

1. 12-14.

I often see players remove the double of 1NT with hands similar to this one. However, you should not feel all that nervous about defending their contract. For his action, North should have 15+ HCP *and* a productive lead to make. You rate to contribute at least a trick, which will suffice to defeat 1NT if partner has his double.

The vote of confidence nets a stellar result for the guys in the white hats, as the hands are:

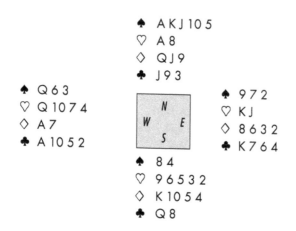

As you can see, while partner has enough for the double, there is no extra fuel in his tank. A top spade followed by a shift to the ◇Q will beat 1NT doubled three tricks, as the defense will then collect five spades, three diamonds and the ♡A.

Proper defensive carding will play a role, needless to say. Some pairs have the agreement that you can lead either the ace or king from ace-king against a notrump contract. The ace is reserved for very good holdings missing only one top honor. Partner is expected to drop an honor if he has one, and give count otherwise. Here, South will play the ♠8, denying the ♠Q and showing an even number of cards in the suit. The opening leader can then try another suit, diamonds in this case, with the hope of getting to partner's hand.

East, meanwhile, chose to stand his ground in 1NT doubled, knowing his side held around half the points in the deck. It was certainly reasonable enough to do so, although it comes to grief here if the opponents defend accurately. The problem from responder's point of view is that there is no clear-cut better spot. As you can see, 2♣ would have gone down only one, but if opener's minor-suit holdings were reversed, that contract would be no bargain either.

CHAPTER 6

CLAIMING YOUR SHARE
OF THE TURF

In the next two chapters, we'll be discussing how to make the right choices when there are at least three and often four players in the bidding, especially at low levels.

Why do some auctions rocket skywards for both sides faster than others? There are two main reasons. The first is that if each partnership has a nine- or ten-card trump fit, they'll be considerably more exuberant in the bidding. The same applies if one player (or more) has a wildly distributional hand. With more balanced hands and minimal eight-card trump fits, the auction tends to move along at a slower pace. The other factor is that in this kind of auction, if the side that is outgunned pointwise also has limited distributional assets, it won't be overly pushy in the bidding as that would be playing with fire.

The recurring theme for most of this chapter will be a variety of doubles and redoubles, used with the intention of gaining the upper hand on the opponents in these low-level struggles for ascendancy.

Embarking on a Hunting Expedition

There are three types of auctions where we can readily identify one side as having the lion's share of the high cards:

LHO	Partner	RHO	You
			1♡
dbl	redbl		

LHO	Partner	RHO	You
			1◇
2◇	dbl		

LHO	Partner	RHO	You
			1♠
2NT	dbl		

Some would consider sequences where a double of 1NT gets left in for penalties to be included in the mix, but we've covered those in Chapter 5.

On these three auctions, opener is presumed to have 12 or more points and responder with his first action is showing 10+ points of his own. So where do we go from here?

The opponents, starting with RHO, who rates to have by far the worst hand at the table, will try and find as safe a haven as they can. Once they settle in their eventual landing spot, your side *as a partnership* will choose from this pair of options:

- Bid on to reach a suitable destination of your own, or...
- Double the opponents for penalties.

Is there a third option? How do you feel about selling out meekly without another peep from either of you? Surely, that isn't part of the equation when you have a comfortable majority of the high-card values in the deck. At least 90% of the time, you'll be able to score a plus on defense or find a decent spot of your own since you aren't forced to go beyond the two- or three-level. The bottom line in all these auctions is that either they get doubled or your side plays the hand. No, there is no Door #3.

Moving on to the specifics, let's continue the first bidding example:

LHO	Partner	RHO	You
			1♡
dbl	redbl	2♣	

As mentioned in Chapter 4, partner advertises 10+ HCP by his redouble. He typically denies a fit for your suit, although he may have a flat hand with barely adequate support. With the same points and extra trump length, he can bid 2NT — this idea also came up Chapter 4, but will be discussed in more detail in Chapter 7.

RHO has now scurried out to his long suit. You are next to speak, and should be guided by the adage that patience is a virtue when making your choice, bearing in mind that if you leave the decision to partner, the opponents' bid cannot be passed out. Moreover, to bid in front of the redoubler without letting him have his say should convey *serious* reservations about the wisdom of defending the hand. Breaking it down with the distribution types outlined in Chapter 1, we'd have the following prescription list:

Hand Pattern	Action
Balanced OR Mildly Unbalanced (5422 or 6322)	You might double if they've bid your four-card suit or repeat a six-card suit if it contains nearly all of your points. Otherwise, you should pass with either of these distributions as responder is obligated to do *something*. You'll therefore have time to show extra length or another suit later on.
Wildly Unbalanced (seven-card suit or 6-5 shape)	Always bid.
Unbalanced (6331, 6421, 5521 or 5530)	Repeat your long suit or bid your other suit.
Unbalanced (5431)	?

Why do I have a question mark beside the 5431 hand pattern? That's because I've said that when opener decides to bid rather than double or pass, he is expressing serious doubts about the idea of defending. To illustrate, let's have a glance at the following hand and the consternation that arose from the bidding:

♠ Q 9 5
♡ K 2
◇ J 9 6
♣ A J 9 6 4

♠ A 8 7
♡ J 8 6 5 2
◇ A K 4 3
♣ 7

Here's what happened to cause the bruised feelings:

West	North	East	South
			1♡
dbl	redbl	2♣	2◇
pass	(snarl)		

Bridge players aren't as innocuous as they look, and our North was mightily peeved at having his blood-lust frustrated.

All joking aside, while opener might rather be declaring the hand, there is nothing from the auction to indicate that his side has a playable fit. Since responder usually has no more than a doubleton heart, you are putting all your eggs in one basket in the hope of a 4-4 diamond fit with 2◇.

From a defensive standpoint, opener's hand is not shabby at all. If partner takes the notion to double 2♣, he has three sure tricks for his side, and how bad can that be? While he might be slightly nervous about how it's going to all turn out, he has enough ammunition at his disposal to pass and then leave in a double of 2♣ if that is responder's decision.

Suppose instead that opener's hand had been:

♠J87 ♡AQ1086 ◇KQJ5 ♣7

With nearly all of his strength located in the core suits and fewer quick tricks on defense, it's more reasonable on this hand for opener to introduce his second suit in front of partner. While responder still won't be happy, a supportive partner will appreciate opener's point of view more in this case than on the earlier hand. Besides, at least North-South are favorites to get a plus score, unlike the other example where opener's 2◇ bid turned a bonanza into a possible minus.

Now we can look at some more hands using the above framework to determine our choice. The auction remains:

LHO	Partner	RHO	You
			1♡
dbl	redbl	2♣	

♠Q1042 ♡AK976 ◇4 ♣A105

Double 2♣ yourself. Prospects on defense are good with a clear-cut lead of the singleton diamond along with first-round trump control. You should be able to negotiate two diamond ruffs along with your side's high-card assets. If you pass rather than double, you might get an unwelcome 2◇ from partner at his turn.

♠A63 ♡KJ865 ◇Q9 ♣K74

Pass. You have a nondescript 13-count and don't want to express an opinion about it one way or the other. Maybe responder will have a better idea of how to proceed than you do. Regardless, you know that he's going to do *something*, as passing out 2♣ is 'verboten' on his part.

♠54 ♡KQJ972 ◇AJ93 ♣8

Bid 2♡. With only one sure trick to contribute, you aren't remotely interested in defending their two-level contract. What, then, to bring into focus — your other suit or the sixth heart? Your major is good enough to play opposite shortness, so mention it again and then show the diamonds next time if you get the chance.

♠J7 ♡KQJ97 ◇AQJ62 ♣5

Bid 2◇. Again your intent is to declare the hand, but here your two suits are of equal length and strength, so give partner the news of your 5-5 distribution.

Redoubler's Continuations

Once responder advertises his 10+ HCP over the double, his next action will clarify his strength and distribution. These are the principles that will apply:

Invitational bids	After the redouble, you can raise opener's suit or bid notrump as cheaply as possible.
One-round force	A subsequent new-suit bid.
Game force	This can be created either by jumping in opener's suit, jumping in notrump, or cuebidding the enemy suit.

Now we can devour some more hands with relish. You're the redoubler this time, and opener has passed in our familiar auction and put the ball in your court.

LHO	Partner	RHO	You
	1♡	dbl	redbl
2♣	pass	pass	?

♠ A Q 9 7   ♡ Q 2   ◇ K J 10 5 4   ♣ 6 3

Bid 2◇, a one-round force.

♠ A K 4   ♡ Q 10 3   ◇ J 7 4 2   ♣ J 9 8

Bid 2♡. This shows a decent 10 to a bad 12 HCP and three-card support. With the same points and four or more hearts, you would have not have redoubled, but opted for 2NT, a conventional raise that will be discussed in the next chapter.

♠ K 8 7 5   ♡ 8 4   ◇ Q 9 6 3 2   ♣ A Q

Bid 2NT. You can't really double 2♣ with only two of them. Although you again have a five-card suit, the two club stoppers are reason enough to try for the notrump game.

♠ A 4 3   ♡ A Q 9   ◇ K Q 8 5   ♣ 10 9 6

Jump to 3♡. Since 2♡ would have been invitational, the jump promises enough values for game.

Card-Showing Doubles

The card-showing double comes up in situations that are similar to the redouble auctions in terms of:

- The values that responder shows, and...
- A hand pattern that has no clear direction, so that it is important to leave several options available for the partnership.

The difference is in the timing, as we can see in these two auctions:

LHO	Partner	RHO	You
			1♠
dbl	redbl		

LHO	Partner	RHO	You
			1◇
pass	1♠	2♡	pass
pass	dbl		

In the first sequence, you know by the first round of bidding with partner's redouble that your side has an advantage in high-card points.

In the second auction, with the interference coming from the fourth player, you cannot tell right away to which side the hand belongs. Partner's 1♠ was forcing for one round but could also have been made on as few as 6 HCP. It takes his second action, the card-showing double, to establish a point-count superiority for your side.

What shape and how good a hand is responder going to have for his card-showing double? The hand will typically be in the 9-11 range, at least three points better than a minimum. The distribution will also be fairly balanced as he hasn't been able to repeat his suit or support opener. The double isn't for penalty; the doubler should, however, be capable of supplying defensive tricks in the event that opener chooses to leave it in.

With the specifics of the card-showing double outlined, we can inspect some hands and decide whether responder should take that path. The auction we'll be faced with is:

LHO	Partner	RHO	You
	1◇	pass	1♠
2♡	pass	pass	?

and we have to decide whether the card-showing double is the right action in each case.

♠Q965 ♡72 ◇KJ94 ♣K103

No. With four-card support and a ruffing value, just compete to 3◇.

♠K8632 ♡A87 ◇85 ♣QJ2

Yes. There might not be a fit in either diamonds or spades. Bidding 2NT is an option, but not a marvelous one, as you could lose the race in trick establishment. Any time 2NT is a make, you may be even better off defending 2♡. This is an ideal hand for a card-showing double, as you have a decent hand pointwise but no overly attractive bid to make.

♠K1097 ♡Q2 ◇1085 ♣AQ64

Yes again. You have 11 HCP but it's a tough hand to describe. It's not enough to force to game, and lacks the heart stopper to invite with 2NT. You do have another suit, but 3♣ would suggest a more unbalanced hand than the collection you actually have. Passing is unthinkable with at least 23 HCP between you, so by process of elimination, double is again what you have left to show the nature of your hand.

All right, so let us now move across the table and put ourselves in opener's shoes, with responder having trotted out the card-showing double. It's one thing to know what it is, but you still have to react appropriately when partner makes one. To recap the bidding so far:

LHO	Partner	RHO	You
			1◇
pass	1♠	2♡	pass
pass	dbl	pass	?

♠AJ4 ♡K6 ◇KJ976 ♣1073

Bid 2♠. Because you didn't rebid 2♠ at your last turn, partner will only expect you to have three of his suit for the delayed raise.

♠Q5 ♡1064 ◇AQJ632 ♣K8

Bid 3◇. In case you're perplexed as to why it took so long to repeat the six-card suit, a free bid at the three-level one round earlier required additional points and/or fewer than seven losers. Now, once partner chimes in a second time, you can show the extra length and he should know from your previous inaction that he is facing a minimum opening bid.

$$\spadesuit A4 \ \heartsuit 95 \ \diamondsuit AQ942 \ \clubsuit K1075$$

Bid 3♣. The strength and distribution of the hand weren't appealing enough to have ventured to the three-level the last time around. Your patience has now borne fruit as partner has made the card-showing double and you can introduce the clubs, to let partner choose between the minor suits.

$$\spadesuit A5 \ \heartsuit K963 \ \diamondsuit AQ97 \ \clubsuit 853$$

Pass and defend 2♡ doubled. RHO might have a reasonable 2♡ overcall, but on this occasion it will turn out to have been an inopportune time for him to step in. Once you lead and continue spades, another round of the suit will promote your ♡9 into a second trump trick. With four or five likely tricks and partner mustering up a second action with his double, the odds are in your favor to leave it in with the expectation of defeating their contract handily.

To sum up, if you are responder and LHO overcalls while opener passes at his second turn, about the only hands on which you'll concede the contract to them are balanced 6- to 8-counts with no support. With attractive distributional features you should bid on and not go quietly. If the assets you're looking at consist of a balanced 9-11 HCP where no particular bid feels right, you can make a card-showing double to announce a better-than-minimum response. You are seeking opener's input in guiding your side to its proper destination.

Responsive Doubles

Another tool that many partnerships include in their competitive bidding toolkit is the **responsive double**. Some auctions commence with an opening bid, a takeout double from partner, and a raise from RHO. You as advancer could pass or bid, but sometimes you have a smattering of values and the desire to compete, but aren't 100% sure of which suit to mention. With these hands, you can make your presence felt via a 'responsive' double. Because the opponents have an eight-card or better fit, this double is for takeout.

Responsive doubles have a sporadic occurrence rate. When partner makes a takeout double, you can safely assume he has good support for the other suits, particularly the unbid major. On most hands of reasonable quality you'll be well-placed to choose the trump suit yourself. However, there are some instances in which you'll need the doubler to cooperate in the selection process.

LHO	Partner	RHO	You
1♡	dbl	2♡	?

♠K974 ♡1065 ◇A873 ♣J3

Do you have an eight-card fit? Yes, absolutely. Where? One thing you can pretty much depend upon when partner makes a takeout double is four-card support for any unbid major. Ergo, your side has enough points and spades to vie for the partscore, and you can get involved by bidding 2♠.

♠Q8 ♡1073 ◇A1087 ♣K964

How about this one? Yes, there will again be an eight-card fit. Partner will have four spades and at most two hearts for his double, so you'll have an adequate trump suit in one of the minors but perhaps not both. Here is the ideal time to make use of the responsive double. This tells partner that you have enough to compete but that you don't have spade length, so he'll head for the better of his minor suits and you'll wind up in the appropriate contract for your side.

Extending the Responsive Double to Overcall Auctions

Although it was originally designed for sequences that begin with a takeout double, a fair number of pairs have expanded the usage of the responsive double to auctions where partner makes an overcall as well. The landscape is similar in some respects but different in others. Suppose the bidding has gone:

LHO	Partner	RHO	You
1◇	2♣	2◇	?

The opponents have a fit and responder has limited his hand, so if you have some points, it makes sense to join the fray. However, it's worth bearing in mind that when partner makes a takeout double to begin with, it increases the likelihood of a fit for your side. When his method of entry is the overcall, he may sometimes have another suit, but that's not a given. This is not to dissuade you from the urge to compete, just a reminder that without a guaranteed fit, you can't afford to skimp on the essentials. Taking this kind of plunge requires a hand that will be comfortable regardless of how the rest of the auction develops.

♠J 1063 ♡AQ94 ◇865 ♣Q9

You can make a responsive double with this hand as there is no downside to speak of. If overcaller bids hearts or spades, you're in clover, while if he repeats his clubs, you've got a top honor in his suit and a side ace-queen for him.

♠A7643 ♡KQ105 ◇982 ♣7

Double. Because of the misfit, this one is kind of dicey. However, overcaller might not have enough values to keep the bidding alive at his turn. If you do elect to get in there, a responsive double is the most flexible choice. Bidding 2♠ may lose a 4-4 heart fit — it may be too risky to introduce hearts later. Harkening back to the 'two bids or one?' theme, your hand only justifies one action. What if overcaller repeats his clubs? Well, it might not be all doom and gloom as you'll be giving him two or three possible tricks.

♠Q7432 ♡KJ85 ◇J97 ♣3

Pass. If you double, how thrilled is partner going to be when he can't do anything other than bid 3♣ and catches this for a dummy? Patience is a virtue with hands like these. If partner has a little bit extra with support for one or both majors, he won't let the bidding peter out at 2◇.

The basics of the responsive double can be summed up as follows:

- It is used in auctions where the opponents have opened and partner has doubled or overcalled.
- For the responsive double to be in effect, RHO has to have supported opener's suit. If he bids a new suit instead, responsive doubles are considered to be *off* unless otherwise agreed.
- If partner has overcalled, the double shows length in the remaining unbid suits.
- If partner has started the ball rolling with a double of a major-suit opening, your responsive double is geared towards locating the best minor-suit fit. If you have points and the other major, just bid it — partner will have four of them.

1) Both sides are vulnerable, and these are your assets:

♠ K Q J 9 2   ♡ Q 7   ♢ A J 10 7 4   ♣ 2

Naturally, you once again have to deal with some interference:

West	North	East	South
		pass	1♠
dbl	redbl	2♣	2♢
pass	2NT	pass	?

Do you like notrump? Should you? And what should be your next bid?

2) Your side is vulnerable, they aren't and you have nothing to write home about:

♠ A Q 10 8   ♡ J 10 2   ♢ Q 5 4   ♣ 10 9 5

You get to respond and then LHO overcalls:

West	North	East	South
	1♣	pass	1♠
2♢	pass	pass	?

Partner hasn't raised our spades or made any further noise. Is it quitting time for us in this auction or not?

3) Instead of some eye-popping distribution, you pick up another *blasé* 9-count for this episode of bidding.

♠ 10 9 7 2 ♡ A Q 9 8 ◇ 8 5 ♣ Q J 3

You are duly greeted with this lively start to the auction:

West	North	East	South
		pass	pass
1◇	2♣	2◇	?

It's nice to have support for partner's suit for once. Does this make the bidding of this hand fairly straightforward?

4) Vulnerable against not yet again, you now have:

♠ K 5 2 ♡ A 7 6 ◇ A 10 4 ♣ 10 9 7 5

It's another decent supporting hand when the opponents interfere:

West	North	East	South
pass	1♠	dbl	?

With invitational values and three of partner's major, what is the best course of action for responder?

QUIZ HAND ANSWERS

1)   Both vul.

♠KQJ92 ♡Q7 ◇AJ10 7 4 ♣2

West	North	East	South
		pass	1♠
dbl	redbl	2♣	2◇
pass	2NT	pass	?

Should you continue describing a 5-5 hand pattern? In bidding 2◇ ahead of the redoubler in a forcing auction, you've already implied an unbalanced hand that isn't terribly keen on defending. Partner has been duly warned and yet has still bid 2NT, which is invitational but passable. With 13 HCP, will game have a decent play?

Whether you take the plunge to 3NT or not in these sequences depends on the quality of your suits, bearing in mind that responder doesn't seem to have a fit for either of them. Here, spades and diamonds are both good enough to provide a source of tricks, so it's reasonable to take the optimistic view of the world.

The whole picture on this deal happens to be:

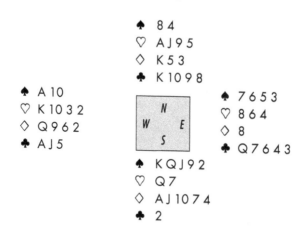

Note that East has a key role to play with his miniscule hand and bids 2♣ at his turn. He's been asked to choose the trump suit and if he has a definite opinion on the matter, should express it as quickly as possible. If he lazily passes instead, West will bid 2◇ or 2♡ and now it's disaster city, as no mercy will be shown by the opponents from that point on.

You can see that 3NT makes handily for North-South: declarer has clubs and hearts well stopped and time to establish tricks in partner's long suits. However, 4♠ can be defeated on a diamond lead and two subsequent ruffs, while 5◊ would lose a trump and two aces.

2)   North-South vul.

♠ A Q 10 8 ♡ J 10 2 ◊ Q 5 4 ♣ 10 9 5

West	North	East	South
	1♣	pass	1♠
2◊	pass	pass	?

With 9 HCP and reasonable spots, you know your side has over half the points in the deck, so it hardly seems right to let them have the contract without contesting the issue any further. The problem is there is no obvious destination for your side to reach. Because of this, many players would pass this hand, not quite sure of what to do. However, that was before we learned about the card-showing double, and this is the perfect hand for it. Whatever opener does, be it repeat his clubs, belatedly support your spades, or leave in the double, your side has a rather good chance of netting a decent score your way.

This action pays off handsomely, as the big picture is:

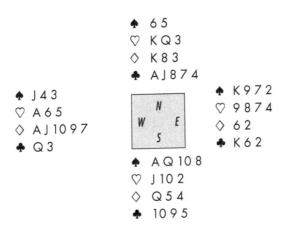

With just a doubleton in partner's suit and four or five tricks of his own, defensive prospects look good enough for opener to sit for the double. Indeed, three rounds of spades provide North with an extra diamond trick, and then he switches to the ♡K. With accurate defense, North-South will rake in two spades, two hearts, a club, and three diamonds for down three on a partscore hand.

Was West's 2◊ that bad a choice? It has some lead-directing value and the colors were favorable for his side, but the unsupported high cards in the black suits won't necessarily translate into winners. I imagine there would certainly be a goodly number of overcallers amongst the bridge populace, and they might get away with it if they were up against a pair that wasn't too familiar with card-showing doubles. But now you're gradually acquiring the tools to make them pay a heavy price on hands like these, and if you get that +500, your LHO will take note that your partnership isn't one he can play fast and loose with.

3)   Neither vul.

♠ 10 9 7 2   ♡ A Q 9 8   ◊ 8 5   ♣ Q J 3

West	North	East	South
		pass	pass
1◊	2♣	2◊	?

With 9 HCP, you have adequate values to bid, and reasonable support for overcaller's suit. There would be nothing wrong with a 3♣ raise, but if you have chosen to play responsive doubles, that enables you to have your cake and eat it too. With this hand you can double to find out whether a major-suit fit exists, as you'll have a respectable dummy for partner regardless of what he does. If he bids hearts or spades, your side hits the jackpot in the higher-paying contract. Nor will you be distraught if he goes back to clubs, as you have good three-card support.

Partner does in fact bid spades and when they persist with 3◊, you can forge ahead in your newly-discovered spade fit without having to venture to the four-level. How will your side fare in 3♠? Quite nicely, as the hand is:

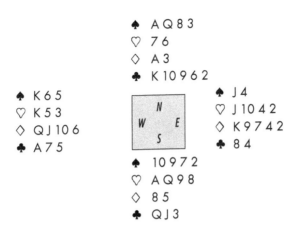

```
                 ♠ A Q 8 3
                 ♡ 7 6
                 ◇ A 3
                 ♣ K 10 9 6 2
  ♠ K 6 5                        ♠ J 4
  ♡ K 5 3          N             ♡ J 10 4 2
  ◇ Q J 10 6    W     E          ◇ K 9 7 4 2
  ♣ A 7 5          S             ♣ 8 4
                 ♠ 10 9 7 2
                 ♡ A Q 9 8
                 ◇ 8 5
                 ♣ Q J 3
```

Playing matchpoints, North-South have to find spades as a possible trump suit to avoid getting a bad score. They can make nine tricks in clubs but not ten, while 3◇ by East-West will go down one or two tricks. In 3♠, declarer (North) can reach dummy with either a club or a heart to finesse the ♠Q and then draw trumps. He'll only lose four tricks in all, one in every suit.

Note that the key to South's taking action was the fact that he had some degree of club fit in addition to both major suits. Even if we turn the third club into a diamond, it would still be a viable option.

4)   North-South vul.

♠K 5 2   ♡A 7 6   ◇A 10 4   ♣10 9 7 5

West	North	East	South
pass	1♠	dbl	?

Limit raises that are offensive in nature are shown immediately, whether or not RHO has bid. Similar values with three-card support are generally shown in a more roundabout way. Here, you can redouble to give a fairly accurate picture of what you have, 10+ HCP with a balanced or semi-balanced hand pattern and the ability to take some tricks on defense. When it's your next turn to bid, you can chime in with a raise if opener hasn't doubled their contract in the meantime.

Defining your hand in this way pays off quite handsomely, as it turns out that even the three-level will not be safe for your side:

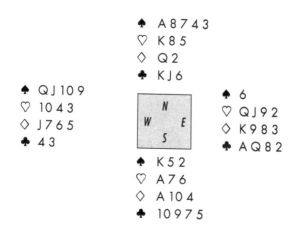

```
              ♠ A 8 7 4 3
              ♡ K 8 5
              ◇ Q 2
              ♣ K J 6
♠ Q J 10 9                        ♠ 6
♡ 10 4 3        N                 ♡ Q J 9 2
◇ J 7 6 5    W     E              ◇ K 9 8 3
♣ 4 3           S                 ♣ A Q 8 2
              ♠ K 5 2
              ♡ A 7 6
              ◇ A 10 4
              ♣ 10 9 7 5
```

Because of the 4-1 trump split, eight tricks are the limit of the hand in spades, and even 2♠ requires careful play to make.

Note that with RHO's double, South is in position to describe his assets with the redouble followed by a bid of 2♠. Also, North should devalue his hand somewhat as the holdings in the side suits don't seem well located. If North-South have the auction to themselves with silent opponents, responder has to commit to the three-level to show his strength.

CHAPTER 7

Navigating in the Stratosphere: High-Level Decisions

As I mentioned in the last chapter, there are two distinct types of competitive environments. We've already looked at sequences where each side has no trump fit or at best a minimal fit, where the auction proceeds at a meandering pace. We can now turn our attention to the scenarios where both sides have good to excellent fits, leading to far more spirited bidding and having to make decisions at a level where the stakes are much higher. I'd like to stress that it's impossible to wind up with a 100% success rate on these calls, so you have to be prepared for the occasional downer regardless of how sensible an action you take on any given hand.

In this chapter, the objective will be to establish a framework of raises in competition that will enable you to achieve the desired result in most cases. It is crucial to be on the same wavelength with partner on which of the raise auctions are suggestive of further action by your side. Every player at some time has had the experience of leaving the final say to partner, knowing that he's going to bid or double. Instead, much to your dismay he passes, since he didn't consider the auction to be forcing in any way, shape or form. In a regular partnership, a little advance discussion will be useful in preparing yourselves for the most common of these situations and avoiding that kind of embarrassment.

I'll also mention some tools that you might want to consider adding, such as fit-showing jumps, lead-directing bids and Lebensohl in weak two-bid auctions. Depending on your preference, you can either add them to your repertoire or leave them by the wayside. The key, of course, is whether you are comfortable with them after trying them on for size.

The Law of Total Tricks: Is It a Cure-All?

Let's start with an idea that can be very helpful in auctions where both sides are bidding and you have to decide whether to sell out or bid one more: the Law of Total Tricks. Despite the impressive title, this isn't a new convention or bidding development — or even a law. It is a formula that tries to predict the number of tricks available to both sides on a deal.

The premise is that for any deal, you take the number of trumps each side has in its best fit and add them together. If you then compare that figure to the total number of tricks the two pairs can make if they were each to play in their best trump fit, the Law says that the two numbers should be (roughly) the same. Or, to put in the form of an equation:

$$N\text{-}S \text{ trumps} + E\text{-}W \text{ trumps} = N\text{-}S \text{ tricks} + E\text{-}W \text{ tricks}$$

The Law of Total Tricks (LoTT) was first described by a Frenchman, Jean-Rene Vernes in the 1950s. It didn't gain widespread recognition and popularity until Larry Cohen made it the centerpiece of his 1992 book, *To Bid or Not to Bid*.

To illustrate how the LoTT principle operates and how it can be helpful for making decisions in some cases, we can examine the following deal:

Dealer West
Neither vul.

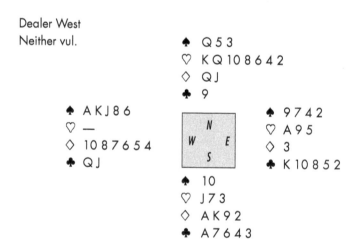

```
                        ♠ Q 5 3
                        ♡ K Q 10 8 6 4 2
                        ◇ Q J
                        ♣ 9
       ♠ A K J 8 6                      ♠ 9 7 4 2
       ♡ —                N            ♡ A 9 5
       ◇ 10 8 7 6 5 4  W     E         ◇ 3
       ♣ Q J               S           ♣ K 10 8 5 2
                        ♠ 10
                        ♡ J 7 3
                        ◇ A K 9 2
                        ♣ A 7 6 4 3
```

Total Trumps: Nineteen (ten hearts for North-South, nine spades for East-West)

Total Tricks: Also Nineteen. Double-dummy, 3♠ for East-West and 4♡ for North-South are the makeable contracts. If the defense leads their singletons in each case, that will be the limit of the hand.

How would the auction go? Typically we'd have something like:

West	North	East	South
1♠	3♡	3♠	4♡
?			

Everyone's initial action is pretty straightforward, so the first real decision occurs at West's second turn. We're now primed to apply LoTT and see what it tells us.

Does opener know for certain how many trumps each side has? Not exactly. Responder could have either three- or four-card support, while South will usually have at least three hearts but might also have bid 4♡ on a very good hand with a doubleton in partner's known long suit. Consequently, the total trumps will probably be eighteen or nineteen. Now we can look at each of the possibilities in turn:

- If there are nineteen total trumps, it's always right for West to bid 4♠, as either his contract will make or theirs will.
- If there are only eighteen total trumps, opener still comes out ahead more often than not by bidding 4♠. He gains when either 4♠ or 4♡ makes and loses only when neither side can make more than nine tricks.

While opener has an approximate count on the number of trumps for each side, another player is even more in the know. South can assume ten hearts for his side and nine-plus spades for theirs, as partner normally wouldn't preempt in hearts holding four spades.

The above deal was a spectacular demonstration of LoTT at the game level, with both partnerships having excellent trump fits and short suits galore. However, you can benefit from LoTT even in partscore auctions. For example, suppose you are South and get dealt this mangy-looking hand, not vulnerable against vulnerable opponents:

♠J76 ♡Q873 ◇943 ♣K75

And the bidding goes:

West	North	East	South
	1♡	1♠	2♡
2♠	pass	pass	?

Your hand is no great shakes for the 2♡ raise, with 6 HCP and the jack of their suit probably a non-value. Moreover, you have the ugly 4333 distribution, which is seldom a positive. Yet LoTT proponents will strongly argue for a 3♡ bid here because of the fourth trump. Why?

What is the total trump count given the bidding so far? Since partner hasn't ventured on to 3♡ himself, he has five and therefore your side has nine hearts. How about the opponents? You're assuming they have eight spades for the time being. The grand total for both sides is seventeen trumps, and the number of total tricks will be the same according to LoTT.

If the hand is a 'match' of trumps and tricks, continuing on to 3♡ should work in your favor. If they can make 2♠, you'll have nine tricks in hearts. If you go down in 3♡, they can make nine tricks in spades but might not bid 3♠, and your -50 will still be preferable to giving up 110 or 140.

Trumps and tricks might not be an exact match on this hand, for reasons that we'll discuss later. However, even if the total tricks are only sixteen rather than seventeen, the vulnerability conditions are so advantageous for our side that it will be generally be right to bid on.

Is taking a further call with this dead minimum for our previous bidding a success or not? Well, this time it happens to be good news for the guys in white hats:

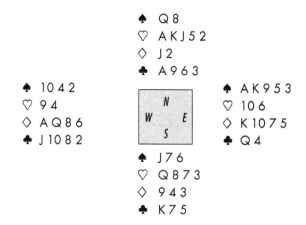

```
                    ♠  Q 8
                    ♡  A K J 5 2
                    ◇  J 2
                    ♣  A 9 6 3
    ♠  10 4 2                        ♠  A K 9 5 3
    ♡  9 4              N            ♡  10 6
    ◇  A Q 8 6      W       E        ◇  K 10 7 5
    ♣  J 10 8 2         S            ♣  Q 4
                    ♠  J 7 6
                    ♡  Q 8 7 3
                    ◇  9 4 3
                    ♣  K 7 5
```

It turns out that LoTT is *not* a precise match on this hand, as there are seventeen trumps (nine for North-South, eight for East-West), but only sixteen total tricks. In fact, 2♠ makes on the nose while 3♡ goes down one. However, that's still a better result for your side than letting them play 2♠. What will East do if you bid 3♡? Some might choose to pass, and others would decide to persist with 3♠. If the overcaller bids on, North-South will now collect a plus for an excellent score.

Note, by the way, that the South hand produces three tricks with hearts as trumps. The ♡Q was known to be useful, and the ♣K was a possible trick. The extra heart kicks in as well because the fourth losing club can be ruffed in dummy.

The Law of Total Tricks is a useful aid, but does have some limitations:

- You can estimate how many trumps each side has based on the auction, but you usually can't really tell for sure.
- Even Cohen, the Law's primary advocate, explained in his book how adjustments need to be made in the LoTT calculation. Trick-taking ability can be reduced if one or both hands contain 4333 distribution, for example. The same applies to hands that consist mainly of queens and jacks. High cards in the opponents' suit tend not to be as valuable than if they were located elsewhere, as partner will likely have shortness opposite them and they may also be worth tricks on defense. Hands with two-suited fits can sometimes produce a lot more tricks than the Law predicts.

These variables affect to some degree the frequency of matches between total trumps and total tricks. Mike Lawrence and Anders Wirgren, in their 2004 analysis (*I Fought the LAW*), state that LoTT produces an exact match on only 35-40% of deals. However, that is by no means a reason to disparage or attach little importance to it. Paul Mendelson's study concludes that the Law is accurate to within one trick on the vast majority of hands. It seems, then, that a definite correlation exists between total tricks and total trumps, although it will not always be an exact one.

What the Law of Total Tricks has generated in the bridge populace is an awareness of how crucial having extra trumps can be during the play of the hand. A nine-card or better trump fit is capable of producing more tricks than an eight-card mesh.

The LoTT functions best when you have those additional trumps combined with promising shape. If one of the hands has shortness in another suit, that makes the outlook even rosier. If *both* hands are unbalanced, the possibilities are often glittering. When each side has these attributes, it may be that both sides can make game.

Having seen how important the quality of the trump fit and the overall distribution appears to be, we can use that as a springboard to the other topics in this chapter, starting with how to raise partner's suit in contested auctions.

Raises in Competition

If you apply the Law to enough deals, it is possible to come up with an interesting conclusion: it is usually safe for your side to bid to the level of its trump fit. In other words, with nine trumps between you, you are safe at the three-level, since even if you are going down, the opponents can make something. As a result, nowadays, there's a fairly decent chance of your being confronted with an auction such as:

LHO	Partner	RHO	You
		1♠	2♡
3♠*			

LHO's 3♠ bid will be explained as showing four-card or longer support and a weak hand. If you go on to ask about responder's point-count, you're apt to get the mildly surprising reply of 0 to 5 HCP. So why has their jump raise magically transformed from a goodish hand of 10-11 points to a preemptive raise once you've overcalled?

The answer stems from the desire to show that pivotal extra trump length whenever possible. Why on earth do it with such meager hands? It enables opener to determine the exact length of the trump fit and which side has the bulk of the values, and to make accurate high-level decisions. The presence of a nine- or ten-card fit may encourage him to bid on, sometimes to make and on other occasions as a sacrifice against a game.

Not everything is altered in the landscape of raises when the opponents enter the proceedings. Let's look at it from the viewpoint of what is different and what remains the same.

WHAT DOESN'T CHANGE

The single raise stays the same — 6-9 points, meaning it is business as usual for the SAYC bidders. That's a slight widening of boundaries for those who play the single raise as constructive, due to the importance of establishing the fit without delay once both sides are in the auction.

It's not a good thing to stretch for a three-card raise. I've seen players make them on 5-counts, and it leads to nothing but trouble, making opener's job way tougher than it has to be. Responder is also entitled to use his judgment on 6-point hands. Suppose partner opens 1♠ and RHO overcalls 2♡. Which of these hands is more promising?

♠Q 10 4   ♡65   ◇9754   ♣A964

♠965   ♡QJ7   ◇10863   ♣K52

The first hand has better trumps, a sure outside trick, and a possible ruffing value in the enemy suit. The second hand might produce only one trick, if that, with the ♣K. With poor trumps, the barren 4333 distribution and the ♡QJx not looking too great for offense, it's by no means an automatic raise.

WHAT SHOULDN'T CHANGE

When our side has a free run in the bidding, the leap to game in opener's suit is typically based on distribution rather than a wealth of high cards. These hands are fairly typical 4♡ bids when partner opens 1♡:

♠ 6 3 ♡ K J 10 8 2 ◇ Q J 7 6 ♣ 10 4

♠ — ♡ A 9 7 6 ◇ 8 5 3 2 ♣ Q 10 7 6 3

♠ 8 ♡ Q 9 6 4 2 ◇ 8 7 6 5 3 ♣ K 5

While there are minor differences between them, they all share the characteristics of being not exactly brimming with points but having plenty of trumps and quite often shortness in a side suit as well. If there happens to be a 1♠ overcall on the right, all of these hands are still 4♡ bids. Responder shouldn't be deterred by the interference, which has actually enhanced the second and third hands.

What a jump to game should *always* show, even in competition, is:

- Fewer than 10 HCP
- Not much in the way of defense
- A very good trump holding and/or unbalanced shape

Ah, you might protest, but then what is responder to do with a hand that wants to be in game with a bunch of high-card values, such as:

♠ A 7 ♡ Q J 5 ◇ A J 10 2 ♣ Q 7 5 4

Well, there *is* a way to show it, as we'll discover shortly.

WHAT CHANGES A LOT

The jump to the three-level is significantly downsized when they overcall or make a takeout double. Instead of 10-11 HCP, it's now a paltry 0-5. The lack of high-card strength is offset by the guarantee of four-card support. The LoTT suggests that you can bid safely to the level of your longest trump fit. So with nine trumps, you can bid to the three-level.

The objective of the weak raise is twofold. You advise opener of a nine-card trump fit for your side, while at the same time denying the opponents the luxury of exchanging information at a more convenient level. For that weak jump raise in competition, again after 1♡ by partner and 1♠ by righty, you could have any of these hands:

♠632 ♡K1087 ◇J942 ♣84

♠5 ♡J963 ◇Q8764 ♣1052

♠864 ♡Q852 ◇854 ♣J97

The first hand is near the top of the 0-5 HCP range, and the second one benefits from having shortness in the enemy suit. The third example requires discussion on how the partnership intends to treat it. Some pairs will elect to go with the preemptive raise if not vulnerable, but pass if they are vulnerable. Others would pass at all vulnerabilities, while an intrepid few would venture 3♡ at all colors. If you adopt the weak jump raise in contested auctions, try to arrive at a decision between the two of you about if and when the last hand qualifies.

HOW DO WE SHOW A BETTER-QUALITY RAISE?

Since all direct raises in competition show 9 or fewer HCP, how do we go about showing the nicer hands of 10 or more? We can adopt the cuebid of their suit for that purpose. It can be made on three- or four-card support, and will show a limit raise *or better* in opener's suit, encompassing all good hands that are willing to agree partner's suit as trump. Harkening back to the auction:

LHO	Partner	RHO	You
	1♡	1♠	?

These hands all meet the standards for a 2♠ cuebid:

♠103 ♡A85 ◇QJ76 ♣A1042

♠A54 ♡KJ63 ◇92 ♣Q986

♠A7 ♡QJ5 ◇AJ102 ♣Q754

The third hand, as you'll recall, is the one where responder's intent is to drive to game in a manner that confirms high-card values rather than extreme shape. Opener will assume the limit raise and might sign off in 3♡, but now with this hand you just continue with 4♡, after which you'll be known to have the better hand.

Sometimes you'll be greeted with a hand that is a fraction short of 10 HCP but which has distributional assets as well. Should it be upgraded to a limit raise? My answer is that partner will expect about one and a half to two defensive tricks for a cuebid. If your hand is in that neighborhood, go for it with the more encouraging bid. If not, content yourself with the single raise and then hope a further chance arises, either by partner or the opponents bidding again.

LHO	Partner	RHO	You
	1♡	1♠	?

♠6 ♡J932 ◇A1064 ♣KJ53

♠9 ♡K65 ◇AJ87 ♣97543

♠9 ♡KJ9 ◇Q954 ♣Q8753

The first hand is worth the cuebid: it has 9 HCP, a fourth trump and a ruffing value in their suit. The next one is more borderline, but a fair number of players would take a rosy view and treat it as a limit raise with some justification. However, that would be way too much of a stretch on the third hand, which lacks surefire tricks on both offense and defense.

We've seen raises made with three and four trumps in the example hands so far. It would be nice to tell partner exactly how many we have every time, but it can't be done. After an overcall, the cuebid is the only forcing bid that immediately advertises a fit. However, when RHO enters the fray with a takeout double, the options for responder increase and you can now make both types of raises. The secret is in how quickly you raise.

As mentioned in the earlier chapters, you can redouble to show 10 or more points. That frees up a 2NT response for other purposes, as most good hands will start with the redouble to see how the auction develops. Many partnerships have the agreement that a jump to 2NT over a takeout double is a conventional raise of opener's suit, to show an invitational or stronger hand. (Like most conventions, it has a name — it is known either as Jordan or Dormer). It will also include better-than-average trump support (at least four cards for a major suit and five cards in a minor). With the same points and one fewer card in opener's suit, you redouble and then show support later.

LHO	Partner	RHO	You
	1♠	dbl	?

♠Q 10 7 6   ♡A 4   ◊J 8 5 2   ♣A 6 3

Bid 2NT, to convey the message of four-plus spades and 10 or more points. Usually, opener will now bid 3♠ or 4♠, but he could also make a game try by bidding a new suit at the three-level.

♠A 9 5   ♡8 7 3   ◊K 6 5 4   ♣K J 2

With just three-card support, redouble with the idea of bidding 2♠ next unless opener doubles them.

♠K Q 8 7   ♡10 2   ◊K J 5 3   ♣A 9 4

Four-card support, so that means 2NT. Even if opener signs off in 3♠, with full opening points you'll carry on to game.

To recap, then, over a takeout double on your right, if you have 10+ HCP:

- With extra trump length, raise immediately via the artificial 2NT.
- With barely adequate trump support, make a delayed raise, by redoubling first and then bidding your partner's suit at the next turn.

POSTSCRIPT

The structure I've described represents the most popular modern approach and owes its popularity to two factors. One is the desire to stir the pot and raise aggressively with outstanding support, even with relatively few points. Much of it was actually suggested prior to the espousal of the Law of Total Tricks, but there were doubts as to its validity. LoTT was the second and more pivotal factor, the clincher that seemed to affirm the framework's merit in the eyes of the bridge public. From the mid-nineties onward, it has rapidly gained momentum in duplicate bridge circles.

In the end, whether you adopt this method is a matter of choice. I'd recommend taking it out for a test drive with an open mind. You can then assess the results and decide whether or not it's your cup of tea. You may delight in this bidding style or elect to retreat back to invitational jump raises. It's up to you.

How to Identify Forcing Situations in a High-Level Auction

When there is a flurry of bidding once each side has agreed on a suit, it signifies the presence of very good trump fits and/or unbalanced distributions at the table. This might occasionally negate even a sizeable advantage in high cards, but shouldn't be a deterrent if you strongly feel the hand belongs to your side.

The problem is that sometimes it's hard to know why they (or you) are attempting to buy the contract. Is it with the expectation of making it, or is it a case of taking a sacrifice? Several articles, and even entire books, such as Andrew Robson's *Partnership Bidding at Bridge — The Contested Auction*, have been devoted to sorting out when these auctions are *forcing* on the partnership to bid further or double the opposing contract.

Rather than try to cover every possibility with a deluge of rules and guidelines, I'll introduce you to the topic via three bidding sequences and we can use logic to decide how the partnership should react to them.

LHO	Partner	RHO	You
			1♡
1♠	4♡	4♠	?

What types of hands do partner and RHO have? As discussed in the previous section, any time responder has 10+ HCP with support, he'll opt for a new suit or a cuebid of their suit, both of which are forcing for one round. In jumping to 4♡, therefore, partner is suggesting 9 or fewer points, hearts galore, and likely ruffing values in a side suit.

What about RHO's 4♠? That is anyone's guess because your side has taken away a fair chunk of his bidding room. He could be bidding it to make his way. Or maybe he thinks he can't defeat 4♡ and is taking a save against it. He might also have a game invite and is now reluctantly taking the push, hoping for the best.

Is your side obliged to do anything further at this point? No, because responder's 4♡, being a distributional raise, does *not* guarantee the majority of high-card points for your side. Besides that, partner should defer to you, so you can now either pass, double, or soldier on to 5♡, as you've got a pretty fair idea of what partner has. By contrast, partner has little idea of what he's facing, other than 5+ hearts and opening values.

LHO	Partner	RHO	You
			1♡
1♠	2♠*	4♠	?

Responder promises more here, as his 2♠ cuebid shows a limit raise or better. That said, his action merely invited game and your side might have ground to a halt in 3♡ if RHO had passed. What is a certainty, though, is that you have more than half of the deck pointwise. East's 4♠ bid could be an advance sacrifice, prompted by the expectation that you'd sail into and make 4♡ your way. However, whether it's a preemptive strike or to make, his vault into 4♠ results in a dilemma for you.

Is this a forcing sequence or not? In other words, if you pass now, does partner have to bid on or double when the auction gets to him? The partnership should discuss auctions that feature a limit raise in competition and establish an agreement on whether or not it creates a force. I treat this auction as forcing because in my regular partnership, opening bids are normally 12+ HCP and we don't skimp on points when making a limit raise. However, pairs who are more aggressive with their opening bids and the hands they consider suitable for an invite might feel differently.

I recently took a poll of experts on this sequence and of the twenty-five replies I got, sixteen said it was forcing, seven considered it to be non-forcing and the other two felt it to be sometimes forcing depending on the vulnerability. In other words, there is by no means a consensus even amongst regular partnerships on this type of auction. Yet such flurries of bidding aren't unusual in a pairs or team game of reasonable quality, so we should address the issue and be prepared when it occurs, rather than be left groping aimlessly.

LHO	Partner	RHO	You
			1♡
1♠	3♠*	4♠	?

Without the overcall, partner's 3♠ would be a splinter raise, advertising shortness in the bid suit, 11-14 HCP, and at least four-card support. Nothing changes with LHO's intervention: the meaning is exactly the same. The question now arises, does *this* generate a bid-or-double obligation for your side once RHO bids 4♠?

The answer here should be a resounding 'Yes'. Why? You have an opening bid opposite a hand that likely also would have opened. Given these circumstances, it makes little sense to acquiesce quietly to the opponents buying the hand. Your side must either persist in your suit or, to quote a friend of mine, 'put the mark of Zorro' on the contract they've landed in.

Now that you're faced with an auction where your side cannot stand by idly, we can see how the process operates for each member of the partnership. If bidding on entailed going to the six-level, control of the opponents' suit would be a key factor. Here, though, the decision revolves around venturing on to five of your suit, and you have to gauge whether your hand is best suited for offense or defense.

The player in direct seat, opener in this particular instance, gets to express his view first. He can:

- bid on to the five-level himself
- double
- pass, leaving the final choice to partner

Bidding and doubling are straightforward, the latter implying that opener feels his side can't go plus at the five-level unless partner has a truly remarkable hand.

It's the meaning of the third option — pass — that is frequently misunderstood. A pass by opener reflects a state of uncertainty on his part, and suggests that he is not wholly confident of a make at the five-level. His hand is probably neutral, with no clear-cut preference between declaring and defending, and he's willing to let it go round to responder and solicit more input from him. He's therefore casting a tentative vote to defend, but not an emphatic one.

That's the theory of the **forcing pass**. As always, it's helpful to take a look at some hands. Let's use the most recent auction for the initial stab at it:

LHO	Partner	RHO	You
			1♡
1♠	3♠*	4♠	?

♠82 ♡KQ1094 ◇QJ ♣AK109

It's useful to count potential losers in these situations, knowing that partner has 11-14 points with 0-1 spades. What can you expect? One loser in spades and none in hearts seem fairly certain. Can you hold your minor-suit losers to one? Yes, in all likelihood, as your honors there will combine nicely with what partner has. You expect to have a good play for eleven tricks and should bid 5♡ yourself.

♠KQJ ♡Q10965 ♢J4 ♣A87

By contrast it is painfully obvious that this hand went down the tubes when partner made the splinter raise. You now have just two cards of value offensively, the ♡Q and the ♣A. The ♠KQJ are only worth anything on defense. You therefore want no part of the five-level and should try and nip in the bud any idea partner has of going there by doubling.

After two hands where opener has a clear-cut preference on whether to play or defend, let us examine this pair of holdings:

♠A8 ♡QJ964 ♢Q5 ♣A943

♠82 ♡QJ964 ♢AQ ♣A943

You have 13 HCP in each case, a minimum opener. Neither of these hands is going to bid 5♡, so that leaves pass or double. Which should it be? And is there any noticeable difference between the two for offensive purposes?

The answer revolves around the location of the pointed-suit ace. When it's in their suit, it represents the same thing in play or defense: one trick. Put it in diamonds, and it enhances the value of the queen, and now all of the points are in suits where responder will have length. The first hand is therefore not so promising and should double. The second hand is a bit more attractive and can pass, leaving responder with the final say.

This deal came up in tournament play, where the opener was actually in possession of the first hand. For his splinter, partner had:

♠5 ♡A875 ♢J7632 ♣KQJ

Opposite opener's hand, there are two quick losers in diamonds and you need the trumps to behave very well to make 5♡. Not so if opener has the second hand, where the chances are much better for your side.

Okay, we've had a look at the whys and wherefores of how to proceed in direct seat. What about when you're the other member of the partnership? Well, you'll often have the benefit of having received partner's vote already. If he's bid on, that's that, unless you want to contemplate going farther still. If his action was double, he's sounded a warning and you should leave it in with any normal hand for your previous bidding. Only if you think you can make more in your agreed suit opposite a dead-minimum hand should you even think about removing.

If partner holds his tongue and their bid rolls around to you, now you're back in the picture with the last say. For our new set of hands, we'll backtrack to the second of our three example auctions:

LHO	Partner	RHO	You
	1♥	1♠	2♠*
4♠	pass	pass	?

Let's say you've hashed it out with partner and decided your side is indeed compelled to do something over 4♠ because of your high-card edge. So here you are following opener's pass, and by agreement you must bid or double at this juncture:

♠4 ♥K986 ◇AJ4 ♣Q10763

Bid 5♥. Partner hasn't doubled, so you're entitled to compete to the five-level if your hand looks promising for offense. Pointwise, you don't have much extra, but there are three pluses that argue in favor of bidding: the fourth trump, the singleton spade, and a five-card suit that might be developed into the tricks you need.

♠AJ ♥KJ52 ◇J763 ♣Q94

Double. You were probably going to force to game, but the values are too soft to make the five-level attractive for your side, even though you have a fourth trump. You can't expect the doubleton spade to be a ruffing value as opener will probably have the same holding in the suit that you do. The outside jacks may not be working cards, and it wouldn't be a surprise to lose a spade and two minor-suit tricks.

♠A63 ♥QJ7 ◇K1095 ♣A108

Bid 5♥ with this hand, as your chances of success are much greater. Why? While the hand doesn't contain extra trump length or unbalanced distribution, the values outside the trump suit are 'pure', i.e. aces and kings. Also, with opener looking as though he has very few spades and length in the minors, the wonderful intermediates you have in those suits could be useful assets in the play of the hand.

Fit-Showing Jumps

The idea of fit-showing jumps (or FSJ for short) arrived on the heels of the Law of Total Tricks and the preemptive jump raise. Due to frequent misunderstandings as to the nature of the beast, the FSJ didn't catch on quite as quickly as the other two concepts, and was used mostly in experienced partnerships rather than 'across the board' by the bridge community at large.

In recent years, though, the fit-showing jump has become more popular and is now acquiring a much broader spectrum of devotees.

Let's use this auction as the springboard for our look into the brave new world:

LHO	Partner	RHO	You
1♠	2♣	3♦	

Prior to the advent of the fit-showing jump, some pairs had the agreement that responder's 3♦ showed a weak hand and a long suit. Others would play it as natural but with a very strong hand. However, neither of these treatments is particularly effective. If you have the weak hand, why give the show away unless you have an active fit for opener's suit? As for the powerhouse, you can bid 2♦ to show a good hand, create a one-round force, and preserve an entire level of bidding space.

Cue the entrance of the fit-showing jump. The gist of it is that any jump in a new suit during a competitive auction would promise a respectable five-card or longer suit *and* at least four-card support for partner. You might make the new-suit jump after a 1♠ opening with something along the lines of:

♠ Q J 9 3   ♡ 10 7 2   ◊ A J 8 7 5   ♣ 6

Before rushing headlong into adopting this tool, however, let's be a bit more specific in its description.

What is a 'respectable' side suit? A six-card suit headed by at least one of the top three honors or a five-card suit of K109xx or better. Lesser five-card suits do not qualify.

What is the expected point-count? It will generally fall in the range of 6-9 HCP. The fit-showing jump resembles in some ways the leap to four of opener's major. While the direct game raise stresses trump length and/or ruffing values, the FSJ identifies a suit that might provide a source of tricks along with good support.

Does it commit the partnership to game or to taking further action if the opponents bid on? No. Responder's bid is severely limited in high cards, so you can stop below game unless the fit jump has been made at the four-level. If the adversaries continue to flail away with their suit, there is no obligation for your side to bid on.

How much defense does the FSJ show? Very little, and preferably none at all outside the two long suits. It is primarily an offensive raise, designed to assist opener in gauging how well the two hands mesh. Since a double fit markedly increases the trick-taking ability, the fit-showing jump is a nice way of determining if one exists.

Are fit jumps restricted to the side that opens the bidding? Not at all — they can also be used after partner has overcalled. An example would be:

LHO	Partner	RHO	You
1♠	2♡	2♠	4♣

Your 4♣ is again fit-showing with 5+ decent clubs and at least four hearts.

Are all new-suit jumps in competition fit-showing? Not quite. Game bids in a new suit are to play and are *not* fit-showing.

There is another jump that falls into the gray area and ought to be discussed before embarking upon your FJS voyage:

LHO	Partner	RHO	You
			1♠
2♣	4♢		

If LHO had passed, partner's 4♢ would have been a splinter raise, 11+ HCP with diamond shortness and 4+ spades.

What's the story, though, when they overcall 2♣? Do you keep 4♢ as a splinter? Or do you adhere to the fit-showing jump principle, but now expect wilder distribution from partner's hand, such as:

$$♠K8653 \quad ♡9 \quad ♢KJ10542 \quad ♣7$$

You could go either way on this decision, but confusion might reign if some of your new-suit jumps are fit-showing while others are splinters.

In most of my partnerships, we have an agreement that eliminates the chances of a mix-up. The precept is that once an auction turns competitive, the only splinter raise that is deemed to be useful is in the enemy suit. All other new-suit jumps below game are fit-showing. With that guideline in place, we'll revert to our now-familiar sequence to view how this treatment operates:

LHO	Partner	RHO	You
	1♠	2♣	?

Besides the raises mentioned earlier in this chapter, you have these options:

3♢, 3♡   Fit-showing jumps.

4♣   Game-going raise with shortness in the opponents' suit.

4◇   Fit-showing rather than a splinter, as the jump is not in overcaller's suit. More extreme shape than its three-level counterpart, usually 10-11 cards in your and opener's suits.

4♡   To play. Remember, game bids in a new suit will be natural, and aren't included in the fit-showing realm.

Now that we have the theory down pat, we can move on to real life. Let's now focus on some example hands and determine what bid responder ought to select after 1♠ from partner and 2♣ from RHO:

♠Q974 ♡103 ◇KQ865 ♣87

Jump to 3◇. An ideal hand for a fit-showing jump, with the high cards concentrated in diamonds and spades. Bidding 3◇ also has good lead-directing value for your side.

♠KJ82 ♡7 ◇J8653 ♣1094

Bid 3♠. The diamonds aren't good enough for a FSJ. The weak jump raise is a more accurate portrayal and denies LHO the ability to introduce hearts conveniently.

♠KQ85 ♡AJ4 ◇Q7432 ♣4

Splinter with 4♣. The good support and distributional control in their suit are the features you want to be showing here. If partner cuebids 4◇, you'll return the favor with 4♡ and let him take it from there.

♠9643 ♡J8 ◇K8532 ♣A7

Raise to 2♠. With the outside ace and poor diamonds, a fit jump wouldn't be a totally accurate bid, while the hand is too good for a weak 3♠ and insufficient for a limit raise. All that's left is the single boost with the intention of accepting any game try that opener makes.

Lead-Directing Bids

Another useful tool that you might have heard of or run into is the **lead-directing bid**. It involves introducing a new suit when it's not very logical to try and play there, either because you already have trump agreement or because partner has shown a good, long suit.

One type of auction that may well see this strategy crop up is when your comrade preempts and RHO bids. Here is a case in point:

LHO	Partner	RHO	You
	2♡	dbl	?

You are in possession of these cards:

♠ 65 ♡ K J 4 ◇ 8 6 4 3 ♣ A Q J 6

The opponents will have 8+ spades between them, and from the looks of it may have some diamond winners available for pitches. You dearly want to attract a club lead from partner, and the good news is that 3♣ is a one-round force as nothing has changed with RHO's double. With luck, either partner or dummy will have the ♣K and you'll be able to snag your tricks in the suit right away.

The lead-directing 3♣ bid is a rousing success as the full deal is:

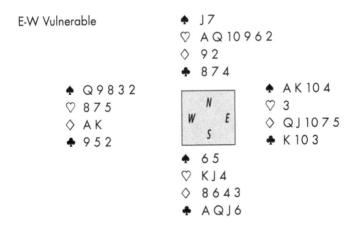

E-W Vulnerable

North:
♠ J 7
♡ A Q 10 9 6 2
◇ 9 2
♣ 8 7 4

West:
♠ Q 9 8 3 2
♡ 8 7 5
◇ A K
♣ 9 5 2

East:
♠ A K 10 4
♡ 3
◇ Q J 10 7 5
♣ K 10 3

South:
♠ 6 5
♡ K J 4
◇ 8 6 4 3
♣ A Q J 6

Without an immediate club lead, West will rake in ten or eleven tricks in a spade contract. Once South bids 3♣, the opponents are destined for a below-average score. North obediently starts out with partner's suit, gets in with a heart and leads another club, taking the first four tricks.

Another situation where you might want to suggest a lead is when both sides have a known fit and you want to lay the groundwork for the most effective defense. Suppose you're greeted by this unfolding of events, with both sides vulnerable:

LHO	Partner	RHO	You
			1♡
1♠	2♡	3♠*	?

and this time you have:

♠ A 5 3 ♡ Q 10 9 8 7 5 ◇ A ♣ K J 6

Partner won't have many of their suit, so this hand is worthy of taking the push to 4♡ with fair expectations of making. If the opponents venture on to 4♠, you want to extract the maximum penalty and a lead-directing 4◇ now will see your side off and running. On a diamond lead won by your singleton ace, you should manage to reach your partner's hand once or twice to score your ruffs. That could well make the difference between a good result and a mediocre to poor one.

Lebensohl over Doubles of Weak Two-Bids

In this day and age of weak two-bids, you'll have many auctions where partner is making his takeout double at a higher level, such as:

LHO	Partner	RHO	You
2♠	dbl	pass	?

and you no longer have a straightforward action as you would over a one-bid. To illustrate, here is a quartet of hands to consider:

a) ♠ 10 5 4 ♡ K J 6 5 ◇ J 7 2 ♣ A 9 3
b) ♠ 9 7 6 ♡ Q 10 8 4 ◇ K 6 5 2 ♣ 10 5
c) ♠ K 9 8 ♡ 6 2 ◇ Q 10 8 7 5 ♣ K Q 4
d) ♠ 8 7 4 3 ♡ J 9 ◇ J 7 6 5 2 ♣ A 4

These would be much easier hands to deal with if the opening bid had been 1♠ and partner doubled. You'd then have a choice of levels at which to show your suit, jumping with the 9-11 point hands.

Here, though, you have no such luxury. Hand (a) isn't strong or distributional enough to venture 4♡. Hand (c) has definite game interest, but a jump to 4◇ bypasses your most likely game in notrump, while bidding 3NT requires partner to have the ◇A or ◇K for that to be a viable contract. Meanwhile, on the other two hands you just want to find a safe landing spot.

Yet if you settle for a three-level bid on all four hands, it leaves the doubler with a pure guess as to whether to go any farther. He won't know if you have a smattering of values or the truly wretched (b) and (d) hands. Bridge players never care to be left groping in the dark, but what's a body to do when there's so little bidding space available?

Eventually, a remedy to this malaise emerged, extending the Lebensohl relay principle to advancer's bidding over a takeout double of a weak two-bid. The theme is familiar if you already play the convention in your notrump environment.

- Direct three-level bids imply hands in the range of 8-11 HCP. Now the doubler can bid or try for game if he has something extra.
- 2NT is a relay to 3♣, which you then pass or correct to your long suit, in this way showing 0-7 HCP. With any normal and minimum takeout double, partner will comply by bidding 3♣ as requested. If he bids something else, you can assume he has a very nice hand, generally 18+ HCP or the equivalent in playing strength.

Using this structure and going back to our four examples, on hands (a) and (c) you can bid your longest suit directly at the three-level, showing respectable values. On their poorer cousins, (b) and (d), use the 2NT mechanism with the idea of showing your suit while denying any game interest.

What is the tradeoff in adopting Lebensohl if the opponents open a weak two-bid? Obviously, you lose the natural 2NT bid over partner's double to show 10-11 points and stoppers in their suit. With this hand, you must either overbid slightly to 3NT or leave in the double. Does it hurt? Maybe occasionally, but the return you get from being able to distinguish poor hands from the slightly more promising ones is ample compensation.

Using Lebensohl if they open 2♡ or 2♠ certainly has some tangible advantages. If they open a weak 2◇, though, it can easily be dispensed with and you can keep 2NT as natural over partner's takeout double, because you now have the two- and three-level available to bid a major.

QUIZ HANDS

1) Nobody is vulnerable and you are South with:

♠K 10 5 2   ♡J 3   ◇A K J 3   ♣6 5 3

The bidding thus far has gone:

West	North	East	South
1♡	1♠	2♡	?

Partner seems to have hit the jackpot with his 1♠ overcall. How do we convey the good news to him?

2) You're vulnerable against not this time, holding:

♠A 9 2   ♡A K 10 8 7   ◇K 9 4   ♣5 4

The auction has skyrocketed in a hurry with:

West	North	East	South
			1♡
2♣	3◇*	5♣	?

Responder's 3◇ was a fit-showing jump, as discussed previously in this chapter. Are you forced to bid on? And should you?

3) With both sides vulnerable, you're greeted by this less-than-inspiring sight:

♠Q 9 2   ♡9 4 3 2   ◇Q 8 5   ♣8 6 5

The opponents get the ball rolling with a weak two-bid and partner can't wait to get in:

West	North	East	South
			pass
2♠	dbl	pass	?

Assume that you and partner have bought into all the stuff that has been introduced in this chapter. What do you bid?

4) Everyone vulnerable once more, you've been dealt this assortment:

♠K 10 4   ♡Q 8 2   ◊J 10   ♣A 9 7 4 3

Partner opens and your RHO has lots to say as the bidding develops:

West	North	East	South
	1♠	dbl	redbl
2♡	2♠	4♡	?

Can your side let them play 4♡ undisturbed, or do you have to double or bid on? With a minimum for your redouble, does your hand justify further action? What kinds of hands do you expect partner and the doubler to have?

5) With neither side vulnerable, you discover that your hand hasn't improved much:

♠8 5 3   ♡J 10 6 5 3   ◊8   ♣A 9 6 5

You get the opportunity to trot out a preemptive raise in competition on this occasion:

West	North	East	South
			pass
1◊	1♡	dbl	3♡*
4◊	4♡	5◊	?

The opponents just can't leave you be. How should you deal with their insistence on playing the hand?

Quiz Hand Answers

1)   Neither vul.

♠ K 10 5 2   ♡ J 3   ◇ A K J 3   ♣ 6 5 3

West	North	East	South
1♡	1♠	2♡	?

This hand is definitely worth a vigorous raise of partner's spades, maybe even all the way to game. However, you'd like to do so in a manner that advertises good high-card strength, and the way to do that is by cuebidding 3♡, showing a limit raise or better. This will set the groundwork for your side to make the winning decision later on in the auction, as the complete deal is:

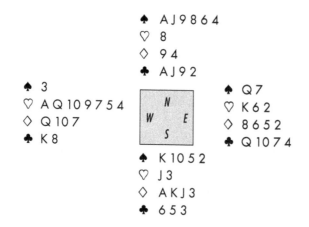

```
              ♠  A J 9 8 6 4
              ♡  8
              ◇  9 4
              ♣  A J 9 2
♠  3                             ♠  Q 7
♡  A Q 10 9 7 5 4      N         ♡  K 6 2
◇  Q 10 7        W        E      ◇  8 6 5 2
♣  K 8                S          ♣  Q 10 7 4
              ♠  K 10 5 2
              ♡  J 3
              ◇  A K J 3
              ♣  6 5 3
```

I'll now show you two auctions. The first one below is how it actually went at the table, and the second one is how it would probably have gone after South had made a 3♡ cuebid.

West	North	East	South
1♡	1♠	2♡	4♠
5♡	5♠	all pass	

West	North	East	South
1♡	1♠	2♡	3♡
pass	4♠	pass	pass
5♡	pass	pass	dbl
all pass			

It was understandable for overcaller to forge on to 5♠ after South's direct game raise, which could (and should) be based on distribution rather than a wealth of high-card points. From North's point of view, he wasn't at all certain of defeating 5♡, while 5♠ could be either a make or a cheap sacrifice.

Now look at our second auction, where South opts for the cuebid to show a limit raise based on high cards. North is able to pass 5♡, having already shown the offensive nature of his hand with the earlier 4♠ bid. With a balanced hand and two likely defensive tricks, South can now double and if they manage the diamond ruff, his side gets to score +500 instead of going minus.

2)   North-South vul.

♠ A 9 2   ♡ A K 10 8 7   ◇ K 9 4   ♣ 5 4

West	North	East	South
			1♡
2♣	3◇*	5♣	?

You'll recall that I asked two questions in the introduction to this hand. First, are you obliged to bid on or double? The answer is 'No', as fit-showing jumps *never* create a forcing situation, as they show distributional hands that are very limited in high-card strength. That said, should you bid on? Will there be a chance to make 5♡ your way? Yes, there is a fairly good possibility of bringing in the red suits without losing a trick, giving you five tricks each in diamonds and hearts plus the ♠A. Taking an optimistic stance is duly rewarded in this case, as the big picture turns out to be:

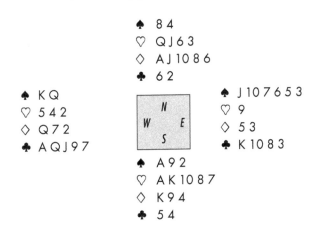

```
              ♠  8 4
              ♡  Q J 6 3
              ◇  A J 10 8 6
              ♣  6 2
♠ K Q                        ♠  J 10 7 6 5 3
♡ 5 4 2          N           ♡  9
◇ Q 7 2       W     E        ◇  5 3
♣ A Q J 9 7      S           ♣  K 10 8 3
              ♠  A 9 2
              ♡  A K 10 8 7
              ◇  K 9 4
              ♣  5 4
```

So 5♣ was a profitable sacrifice their way, down only a couple. Meanwhile, 5♡ needs the diamonds to come home for five tricks. Given East's jump to 5♣, he is more likely to be short in the red suits, and declarer will (successfully) play West for the ◇Q.

Note how effectively the fit-showing jump works in this instance. The contract would probably be 5♣ doubled if opener didn't know there was an outside source of tricks in responder's hand.

3)   Both vul.

♠ Q 9 2   ♡ 9 4 3 2   ◇ Q 8 5   ♣ 8 6 5

West	North	East	South
			pass
2♠	dbl	pass	?

Hearts is your four-card suit, and that's where you'll be heading. Playing Lebensohl over weak two-bids, you have the opportunity to convey the message that your hand is rather threadbare. Over the double, you bid 2NT, asking partner to bid 3♣. With your subsequent 3♡, you show 0-7 HCP and warn him not to entertain thoughts of game. With a hand of 8-11 HCP, you'd have bid a direct 3♡, while 12 or more is enough to commit the hand to game. The Lebensohl treatment comes in handy here, as it saves partner a lot of agony on what to do with his hand:

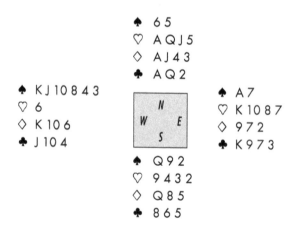

North will still be tempted to bid 4♡ on his 18-count, but with you showing 0-7 points, there's virtually no chance that enough of his six losers will be covered. As you can see, if North-South reach game, it will be greeted with a double by the East hand.

4)   Both vul.

♠ K 10 4 ♡ Q 8 2 ◇ J 10 ♣ A 9 7 4 3

West	North	East	South
	1♠	dbl	redbl
2♡	2♠	4♡	?

Since you have 10 HCP facing partner's opening bid, you as a partnership have to do *something* over their 4♡ contract, either bid on or double. So what to do here — take the bull by the horns or leave it for partner to express his desire? Well, there are a fair number of clues from the bidding thus far. Given partner's rebid and RHO's leap to 4♡, opener will have 6+ spades and short hearts as well. You don't have too much wastage in hearts, and both the five clubs and doubleton diamond may be useful in a spade contract. Your hand should offer a good play for 4♠, and that's how you should proceed. There should be a happy ending to this story, as witness:

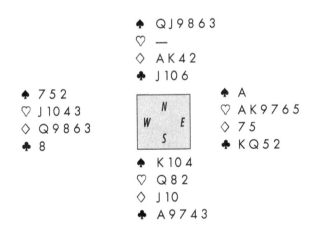

```
            ♠ Q J 9 8 6 3
            ♡ —
            ◇ A K 4 2
            ♣ J 10 6
♠ 7 5 2                      ♠ A
♡ J 10 4 3      N            ♡ A K 9 7 6 5
◇ Q 9 8 6 3  W     E         ◇ 7 5
♣ 8             S            ♣ K Q 5 2
            ♠ K 10 4
            ♡ Q 8 2
            ◇ J 10
            ♣ A 9 7 4 3
```

Even if East leads the ♣K and eventually gives West a ruff, the best the defense can manage is three tricks. So what's the problem, you may ask? Well, here's how the auction actually finished up:

West	North	East	South
	1♠	dbl	redbl
2♡	2♠	4♡	pass
pass	pass!		

After South passed, opener was left between a rock and a hard place. He'd advertised extra spade length by mentioning them again and responder didn't seem interested, so he gave it up, despite realizing that it was a no-no. This led to major fireworks in the post-mortem, after they collected a mere +100 against 4♡ instead of the +620 they were entitled to.

The Bridge World magazine used to have a feature called 'You Be the Judge' where a panel of experts would adjudicate a bidding or defensive carding mishap. They would be asked to apportion the blame and name the worst single action. I'd guess they would agree that opener can't pass 4♡ (although there would be varying opinions on what to do instead), and a few might have preferred 3◇ instead of 2♠ at opener's second turn. Still, they would come down much harder on South, who knew there was a fit and also that partner was short in hearts, but neglected to bid 4♠, creating an unnecessary problem for opener.

5)   Neither vul.

♠ 8 5 3   ♡ J 10 6 5 3   ◇ 8   ♣ A 9 6 5

West	North	East	South
			pass
1◇	1♡	dbl	3♡*
4◇	4♡	5◇	?

This is one of those hands where you have to resist the temptation to bid again, despite the known ten-card heart fit. Having made a preemptive raise, South has described the type of hand he has and should now pass, allowing overcaller to have his say. In fact, it's closer to a double than a bid, as you have one defensive trick more than you could have. One essential in keeping partnership morale high is not telling your story twice.

Alas, when this hand was played, our South went on to 5♡ and this was the layout of the cards:

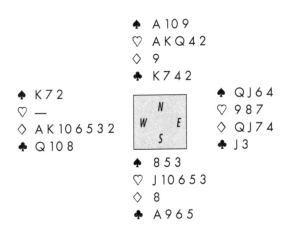

♠ A 10 9
♡ A K Q 4 2
♢ 9
♣ K 7 4 2

♠ K 7 2
♡ —
♢ A K 10 6 5 3 2
♣ Q 10 8

♠ Q J 6 4
♡ 9 8 7
♢ Q J 7 4
♣ J 3

♠ 8 5 3
♡ J 10 6 5 3
♢ 8
♣ A 9 6 5

North might not have doubled 5◇ if South had passed, but it's unlikely he would have bid on with fair expectations of three tricks on defense. The East-West game is shy a trick, whereas you are two in the glue in a 5♡ contract.

CHAPTER 8

Six Partnership Discussion Topics

Partnerships, even regular ones, will sometimes get their wires crossed and have a mishap on an auction you'd think would be fairly straightforward. The explanation is frequently that they have decided to include a convention or treatment in their repertoire, but left some aspects of it without discussion.

To take an example, nearly everyone plays negative doubles, but do you have solid agreements on the meanings of responder's next bid? Similarly, you might have filled out your convention card by ticking the box for 'systems on' after a direct notrump overcall, but will that also be in effect following a *balancing* notrump? You may assume it will be business as usual, but some players will drop the system in this case and revert to natural bidding.

Another issue partnerships should cover in some detail but often don't is that of third-seat openings. Do you and partner have the same tendencies or are they quite a bit different? A lot of players adopt Drury — should you do likewise? If so, did you know that there are several variations of it? Which is best, and more importantly, which is a good fit with your style?

In this chapter, I'll bring up a half-dozen such topics that merit discussion in both new and existing partnerships. The time spent firming up your understandings in these commonplace auctions will benefit you greatly as it will no longer be a struggle to interpret partner's bids.

Negative Doubles 201

Way back in Chapter 1, I explained the basics of the negative double structure. Because I didn't want to engage in information overload at that juncture, I left a couple of wrinkles out of the picture. These extensions of the negative double will be more understandable with the knowledge that has been gained in the intervening chapters.

I'll begin with a hand where you as responder have a long suit but no convenient way to show it because of a shortage in points:

♠ Q 10 7 6 4 3   ♡ 7 2   ♢ A J 9   ♣ J 8

The bidding commences with:

LHO	Partner	RHO	You
1♡	2♣	?	

You'd like to bid 2♠ — but oh, fudge: a new suit is forcing in competition and if it's bid at the two-level, it promises 10+ HCP. Opener will likely get carried away and maybe drive the hand to game as he is expecting more values than you actually have.

What about pass, then, hoping that partner is able to keep the bidding alive? The problem is that he'll only do that if he has shortness in the enemy suit *and* adequate support for the unbid suits. Partner might easily have three-plus clubs and a doubleton spade, so you can't count on any further noise from him.

Yet it grates to sell out meekly to the overcall. Is there any solution? Yes, if partner happens to be on the same wavelength. You can make a negative double and *then* bid 2♠ unless opener bid spades first. Opener will know that your hand is in the 6-9 range (probably more like 8-9) and that you couldn't bid the suit directly because your hand wasn't strong enough. Of course, having advance discussion is preferable, but I'm certain that many pairs get to talking about situations like these only after some of them have occurred.

On the flip side, will responder ever make a negative double on a hand with full opening values? Yes, but only if it's the best way of describing the hand. As helpful as they can be, the eternal trap with conventions is that of over-using them when you have perfectly logical natural bids available. To illustrate which of the two is preferable, we can view some more hands with this auction as our backdrop:

LHO	Partner	RHO	You
1♣	2♢	?	

How do you proceed with each of the following hands?

♠ K Q 9 4   ♡ A 10 8 6   ♢ A 3   ♣ Q 4 2

Double, because you're prepared for anything. You'll raise either major or 2NT to game, and bid 3NT if opener repeats his clubs.

♠ K Q 9 4 ♡ A Q 10 8 6 ◇ A 3 ♣ 4 2

Now there is no reason to avoid the simple and natural 2♡. Partner will bid spades if he has them — they won't get lost. A negative double with this hand would be convention abuse.

Responder has several ways of creating a game force after making a negative double if he is still in doubt as to what the final contract should be. Here is a summary of the 'extras' that can be added to the negative double framework:

- A negative double followed by a new suit at the cheapest level below game is non-forcing, showing a long suit and fewer than 10 HCP. Responder doesn't guarantee length in the unbid suit.
- A cuebid of the opponents' suit after a negative double creates a forcing auction. Responder could have a variety of hands.
- A negative double followed by a *jump* in a new suit won't occur that often as responder had the option of bidding the hand naturally. However, it should also confirm game values and both previously unbid suits — responder is longer in the one he bids.

'System On' — Yes or No?

In the last ten or fifteen years, in my experience, there has been no contest in identifying the most prevalent misunderstanding that occurs at the bridge table. It occurs when the opponents interfere over 1NT and one member of the partnership bids naturally, while the other treats the auction as though the system that is normally used is still on.

HOW TO RESOLVE THE UNCERTAINTY

To begin with, not everyone chooses to keep systems on after interference, so don't assume anything and be sure to consult with your partner on the matter. The opponents nowadays are getting friskier all the time, even over 1NT openings, so it's a situation you'll have to deal with time and again.

I have a simple agreement with most of my partners that eliminates potential mixups. It depends on how much of your two-level space their bid chews up. If the overcall has no effect, then you can keep your structure intact. If some of it has been taken away, you should then go natural in your own bidding. The principle can be better illustrated by a glance at this trio of auctions:

LHO	Partner	RHO	You
	1NT	dbl*	?

They are playing DONT, with RHO's double showing any one-suited hand. As responder, you have the entire gamut of bids available, so system is on.

LHO	Partner	RHO	You
	1NT	2♣*	?

Still with DONT, RHO is now promising clubs and a higher suit. As responder, you can still have it all, with double being Stayman and all other conventions remaining in place.

LHO	Partner	RHO	You
	1NT	2◊	?

You've now lost 2♣ Stayman because RHO has bid past it. Accordingly, the system should be discarded in favor of natural bidding. A cuebid would be game-forcing Stayman and the Lebensohl 2NT can be incorporated if you so wish.

In my experience, I've found this operates rather well and doesn't strain the memory unduly. All it takes is the recognition of the following two scenarios:

- If you can have it all despite their interference, system is *on*.
- If you no longer have some of the two-level bids available, then system is *off*.

WHAT'S THE SCOOP WHEN *WE* MAKE A 1NT OVERCALL?

It's also worth taking a minute or two with partner just to make sure you're on the same page when they open and your side overcalls notrump. Here are four auctions in which there is room for the partnership to use the Stayman/transfer repertoire:

LHO	Partner	RHO	You
1◊	1NT	pass	?

LHO	Partner	RHO	You
2♡	2NT	pass	?

LHO	Partner	RHO	You
		2♠	pass
pass	2NT	pass	?

LHO	Partner	RHO	You
		1♡	pass
pass	1NT	pass	?

In the first two examples, you'd expect 15-18 for the direct notrump overcall and therefore 'system on' should definitely apply: you want partner to declare the major-suit contracts as he is likely to have more of the points.

In the third auction, partner has acted in balancing chair but still rates to have around 14-16 HCP as he is endeavoring to take eight tricks in notrump. Once again, 'system on' seems the logical way to go.

In the fourth of our sequences, partner is showing minimum opening values of 11-14 for his balancing 1NT. This is the one where opinions might differ. Some players like to take the system off, the reason being that it will frequently be a partscore hand with your not having bid directly. This would now enable you to use 2♣ and 2◊ as natural and to play. Others might prefer to keep the structure intact and not deviate from it.

The key throughout all of this is not to take anything for granted. You need to deal with each of these scenarios with your partner since they are fairly common occurrences.

'Free' Acceptances of Transfers over a Double

Another situation that crops up regularly is when the opponents double a Jacoby transfer bid. Should opener just ignore it and do as he's been told, or does it create an opportunity that he can utilize to clarify his holding in responder's major?

Let us consider this transfer auction:

LHO	Partner	RHO	You
	1NT	pass	2♡*
dbl	?		

Opener could just bid 2♠ at this point. But wouldn't it be nice to be able to show three or four of them as opposed to a mere doubleton? Since he can now pass without it ending the auction, some pairs decide to have the 'free' 2♠ show outright support and confirm at least an eight-card fit. With only two spades, he would pass instead. This could make a difference if responder was unsure of what to do next after transferring to his major.

Sounds good in theory, you retort, but doesn't that leave responder having to bid his suit and declare the hand when opener passes and the double comes around to him? No, because there is still a way to force opener to accept the transfer. The bidding would continue:

LHO	Partner	RHO	You
	1NT	pass	2♥*
dbl	pass	pass	redbl
pass	2♠		

The redouble is not to play but an insistence that opener now complete the transfer with 2♠.

The 'free bid' idea over the double gives your side a chance to distinguish between actual support and a lesser holding in responder's major. If you combine it with the redouble, which forces acceptance of the transfer after opener has passed, some crucial extra knowledge will often be gained.

If you're intrigued by this concept and feel that it's worth trying, run it by your partner to see what he thinks. He may feel likewise, or throw a damper on the notion, but at least you're in the process of exploring what's out there together.

Drury by a Passed Hand Responder

Even those of you who have never played Drury probably recognize the name and might be somewhat familiar with the gist of it. The idea is that when 1♥ or 1♠ is opened in third or fourth seat, responder can bid an artificial 2♣ with a hand on which he would normally make a limit raise so that you can stay at the two-level if partner is minimum or light for his opening.

Should your partnership adopt Drury? It all depends on how sound your third-seat openers are. If they are still fairly respectable, with any shortage in points being compensated for by unbalanced distribution, there is no urgency to sacrifice a natural 2♣ response in favor of Drury. However, if you are fond of opening a major for lead-directing or obstructive purposes on as few as 9-10 HCP and balanced shape, then you should have a braking mechanism to avoid getting too high when partner has a nice supporting hand. Once again, it's best for you and partner to assess your tendencies as that will answer the question of whether you need to have Drury in your toolkit.

HOW GOOD A HAND WILL RESPONDER HAVE FOR A DRURY 2♣?

He'll have enough to have made a limit raise, and perhaps even a hand that revalues to an opening bid because of attractive distributional features. If partner had opened 1♡, any of these hands would suffice for the bid:

♠J4 ♡AQ5 ◇A1086 ♣7543

♠A9 ♡J1074 ◇KQ82 ♣976

♠K965 ♡AQ42 ◇J653 ♣7

ORIGINAL DRURY

As conventions go, Drury is fairly ancient, dating back to the mid-1950s. However, there have been numerous modifications proposed to it that are of more recent vintage. When the convention made its first appearance, this was how it operated:

Opener	Responder
	pass
1♡	2♣*
?	

Opener then described the quality of his hand, bidding an artificial 2◇ to warn responder of a minimum or sub-minimum. All other bids were natural and promised sound opening values.

REVERSE DRURY

The first 'tweak' that was proposed to Drury was to show a light third-seat opener by simply returning to the known fit, 2♡ in this case. That freed up 2◇ as a natural bid that also shows a reasonable hand. Essentially, in Reverse Drury, there are no artificial rebids by opener, and some people view it as a slight improvement.

MODIFIED REVERSE DRURY

The principle of Reverse Drury is retained, but 2◊ now goes back to having an artificial meaning. Here's the scoop:

Opener	Responder
	pass
1♡	2♣
?	

Now opener's rebids would be:

2♡	Dead-minimum or even lighter hand.
2◊	Sound opening values but only a four-card heart suit.
Anything else	Decent hand, guaranteeing five or more hearts.

This version is worth considering if both members of the partnership might sometimes choose to open a good four-card major in third or fourth seat. You wouldn't need to bother with it, though, if your major-suit openings are always at least a five-card suit regardless of position.

TWO-WAY DRURY

This came along in the early 1990s, when the importance showing four-card raises was being proclaimed by the LoTT disciples. In Two-way Drury, both the 2♣ and 2◊ responses by a passed hand are now used as supporting gestures for opener's major. Within this framework, there are three variations that I know of:

Response	Two-Way	Reverse Two-way	Modified Reverse Two-way
2♣	three-card limit raise	four-card limit raise	four-card raise, can be constructive or limit, with 2◊ by opener asking which it is.
2◊	four-card limit raise	three-card limit raise	three-card limit raise

Partnerships should discuss and evaluate the trade-off when contemplating the move to two-way Drury. Is the gain of distinguishing between three- and four-support worth having to give up natural two-level responses in both minors by a passed hand?

Jump Shifts by a Passed Hand

Weak jump shifts by a passed hand opposite a third-seat opener aren't terribly practical. By contrast, on occasion, when partner opens a major in third seat, your hand becomes so good that you'd dearly like to raise him to four even though you aren't really supposed to. Suppose partner opens 1♡ in third seat and you have these cards:

♠J87 ♡KJ95 ♢AJ984 ♣3

The best way to describe the nature of this hand, *if* you and partner have broached the subject, is to jump to 3♢. It's the fit-showing jump concept all over again, but with a few extra points compared to the hand you'd have in competition. You're confirming great support, a five-card suit worth mentioning, and likely shortness in one of the other suits. Even if partner has a minimum opener, he could still bid game if he has good fitting cards and no black-suit wastage.

When is a Cuebid not a Cuebid?

Sometimes you might have the experience of wanting to open the bidding in a suit only to have an opponent bid it in front of you. Suppose your RHO gets the ball rolling with 1♣ and your hand is:

♠64 ♡A9 ♢AJ10 ♣KJ10975

It's quite irritating, to say the least, as you were about to open and repeat the clubs to show a good, long suit. Since double is takeout and 2♣ would be Michaels to show both majors, you have no immediate way to describe your hand.

Similarly, responder might have introduced a suit you had every intention of bidding. If the auction has gone:

LHO	Partner	RHO	You
1♣	pass	1♡	?

And your hand is:

♠7 ♡AQJ986 ♢AK108 ♣53

You would have gladly opened in hearts and continued to bid aggressively with this five-loser hand. Even if RHO had opened 1♠, you would have overcalled 2♡ and later possibly introduced diamonds. Instead, you've had two bids in front of you and one of the opponents has rudely mentioned your primary suit. The grand scheme of showing 6-4 in the red suits has seemingly been thwarted. Even so, you still have the itch to enter the bidding. Is there *any* way to show these types of hands?

Yes, there is. For a bid of their suit to be natural rather than a two-suited overcall, these conditions have to be met:

- Partner has not yet taken a bid.
- The 'cuebid' is delayed or you had the Sandwich 1NT available at your turn.

We can now survey a few auctions to watch how the principle operates:

LHO	Partner	RHO	You
		1♣	pass
1♢	pass	1♠	2♣

Your 2♣ is to play, as both conditions for it to be natural apply. Your bid of their suit is delayed and there hasn't been a peep out of partner.

LHO	Partner	RHO	You
1♣	1♡	1♠	2♣

Things have changed now that partner has overcalled, as you need the cuebid as a way to show a good supporting hand.

LHO	Partner	RHO	You
1♣	pass	1♡	2♣ or 2♡

Here you have two takeout actions at your disposal with the double and the Sandwich 1NT. Because of this, you don't require either of the 'cuebids' for those purposes and so both 2♣ and 2♡ can function as natural overcalls. If you scroll up to our two conditions, they are both met in this sequence.

QUIZ HANDS

1) With neither side vulnerable, you have this red-suited hand:

♠ 4 3   ♡ Q 10 6 5 4 3   ◇ A Q 8 3   ♣ 9

Naturally, the opponents make it tough for you as the bidding goes:

West	North	East	South
	1♣	2♠	?

With attractive shape but limited points and no fit for opener's suit, is there any feasible course for you to take as responder?

2) You are vulnerable and they aren't, and you have these cards:

♠ Q J 9 7   ♡ J 8 2   ◇ 5 2   ♣ A Q 10 3

Two passes and a third-seat opening later, it's your move:

West	North	East	South
			pass
pass	1♡	pass	?

Drury happens to be in your toolkit, so you have 2♣ available to show a good heart raise. Does this hand qualify?

3) Neither side is vulnerable:

♠ 6 2   ♡ A 9 8 3 2   ◇ K 10 4   ♣ Q 9 5

A rather ordinary hand, but you have somewhat of a coin-toss awaiting you when partner balances over their weak two-bid:

West	North	East	South
		2♠	pass
pass	2NT	pass	?

North is showing a good 14 to 17 HCP for his 2NT in passout seat. Do you have sufficient assets to justify going any further?

4) Neither side is vulnerable.

♠ K J 8 7 4   ♡ 7   ◇ K 10 6 5 2   ♣ 10 7

For once, there's no immediate bidding by the opponents as the auction goes:

West	North	East	South
	1NT	pass	2♡*
dbl	2♠	pass	?

Do you get ambitious with this 7-count or not?

5) Vulnerable against not, you've been dealt:

♠ J 5 4 2   ♡ A J 7   ◇ A 10 7 6 2   ♣ 7

After a couple of passes, partner opens in a suit that is very much to your liking:

West	North	East	South
			pass
pass	1♠	pass	?

Your hand has shot up in value, but partner could be light for his third-seat action. How carried away should you get with these baubles? The two of you have agreed to play Reverse Drury in this situation, by the way.

QUIZ HAND ANSWERS

1) Neither vul.

♠ 43   ♡ Q 10 6 5 4 3   ◇ A Q 8 3   ♣ 9

West	North	East	South
	1♣	2♠	?

The problem on this hand is that you'd like to get to hearts, but 3♡ would be forcing and could get your side too high. How to cut this Gordian Knot?

Thanks to the negative double, there is a way to satisfy the zest to compete and yet not mislead partner about your point-count. You can start off by making a negative double, with the idea of bidding hearts next. Opener will know that you have a long suit but not enough points to make the immediate three-level bid.

What if partner bids 3◇ over your double? The chances of a heart fit would be greatly diminished with his having at least nine minor-suit cards, so you'll be better off most times to pass and remain in the known diamond fit.

What is the outcome of a negative double followed by a heart bid? Pretty good, as the complete deal is:

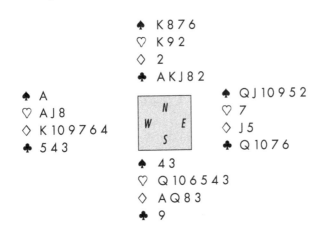

```
                 ♠ K 8 7 6
                 ♡ K 9 2
                 ◇ 2
                 ♣ A K J 8 2
  ♠ A                          ♠ Q J 10 9 5 2
  ♡ A J 8          N           ♡ 7
  ◇ K 10 9 7 6 4  W   E        ◇ J 5
  ♣ 5 4 3          S           ♣ Q 10 7 6
                 ♠ 4 3
                 ♡ Q 10 6 5 4 3
                 ◇ A Q 8 3
                 ♣ 9
```

With a singleton diamond, North will probably avoid notrump and repeat the clubs over South's double. He'll then pass 3♡, figuring his ♠K is misplaced. Declarer can get a crossruff of sorts going, but will eventually run out of gas at nine tricks.

Had South bid 3♡ directly over 2♠, it would have been forcing and opener would have been obliged to raise to the doomed game.

2) North-South vul.

♠ Q J 9 7   ♡ J 8 2   ◇ 5 2   ♣ A Q 10 3

West	North	East	South
			pass
pass	1♡	pass	?

Is this collection worth a Drury 2♣? Yes, just barely. With a respectable 10-count and three-card support, that should be your choice. This hand's points are concentrated in the long suits and it has a ruffing value, so it meets the criteria.

Opener will rebid 2♡ to show no game interest and this hand has no further ambitions since it is rock-bottom for the invite. You wind up in a dandy spot, as partner selected his best suit for his third-seat opening:

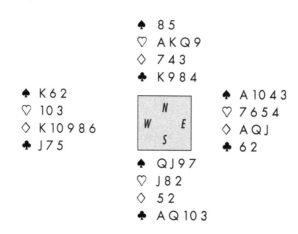

If the opening had been 1♣, East could have got in with a takeout double and West could compete all the way to 3◇ if need be with the colors in his favor. Once North ventures forth with the chunky four-bagger in hearts, though, the opponents are stymied. East is too short in clubs to make a takeout double and has to pass. West has a five-card diamond suit but nowhere close to enough points to bid. Your side gets to play 2♡, making nine tricks for the best possible result.

If you have five-card majors ingrained in your mentality, it's tough to vary from that, even in third seat. Take my word for it, though, when you have a fine suit like this one, it leads to many a good result, particularly when you have Drury in your toolkit to avoid getting overboard.

3)   Neither vul.

♠ 6 2   ♡ A 9 8 3 2   ◇ K 10 4   ♣ Q 9 5

West	North	East	South
		2♠	pass
pass	2NT	pass	?

Balancing notrump actions aren't quite as strong as their direct-seat counterparts (1NT in passout chair can be as few as 11-14). Here, partner is going to be one level higher, so his assets won't be that meager. There are some minor variances, but most pairs adopt a range close to my suggestion of 14-17.

With no room to invite, you have to decide whether to settle for a partscore or bid game. The form of the game is a consideration, because at matchpoints you don't necessarily want to be stretching for contracts that are thin on points, but at teams, with the high reward you get for a vulnerable game, it's a different story.

What's good about this hand? The five-card heart suit is a plus, and your outside king and queen have good chances of taking tricks, as you'd expect the missing honors to be with partner or West rather than in the weak-two bidder's hand. Also, partner could be on the high end of his bid — it's been known to happen.

If you elect to head towards game, what is the best way to proceed? You'd like to offer a partner a choice between 4♡ and 3NT, so the first order of business is to bid 3◇ as a transfer to hearts. Then you'll follow up with 3NT, whereupon North will look at his heart holding and pass or convert to 4♡. If the two of you have engaged in the six-point discussion from this chapter, he'll recognize that it's 'system on' as you have all of it available at the three-level.

Do you come up roses on the push to game? On this occasion, fortune smiles:

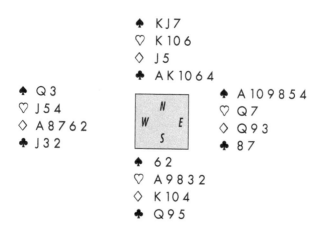

                    ♠ K J 7
                    ♡ K 10 6
                    ◇ J 5
                    ♣ A K 10 6 4

♠ Q 3   ♠ A 10 9 8 5 4
♡ J 5 4   N   ♡ Q 7
◇ A 8 7 6 2   W   E   ◇ Q 9 3
♣ J 3 2   S   ♣ 8 7

                    ♠ 6 2
                    ♡ A 9 8 3 2
                    ◇ K 10 4
                    ♣ Q 9 5

Your 4♡ makes, despite partner having only 15 HCP, due to your having a fit in two suits. You need a little help, but on the bidding you can guess both spades and diamonds, and hearts and clubs also break 3-2, so all's well that ends well. True, partner might not always have three of your hearts and a source of tricks, but when he doesn't, he's just as apt to be at the top instead of the low end of his 14-17 range.

4)   Neither vul.

        ♠K J 8 7 4   ♡7   ◇K 10 6 5 2   ♣10 7

West	North	East	South
	1NT	pass	2♡*
dbl	2♠	pass	?

If West had passed, you would have several options, none of them entirely descriptive of what you have. There are two invitational bids, but partner would expect a more balanced hand for 2NT and a six-card suit for 3♠. If you bid 3◇ instead, that is more accurate shapewise but also creates a game force, and if partner were now to bid 3NT, you'd be stuck in an undesirable contract as he'd only have two spades.

Once LHO doubles, this simplifies the bidding if you and partner have gone over the material in this chapter together. Now that partner has accepted the transfer over the double, he shows at least three of them and you have an eight-card or better fit. This should be enough incentive for you at least to invite with 3♠. Partner will accept and the results are to your liking:

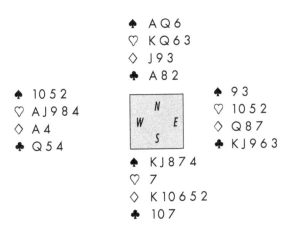

```
                    ♠ A Q 6
                    ♡ K Q 6 3
                    ◇ J 9 3
                    ♣ A 8 2
  ♠ 1 0 5 2                            ♠ 9 3
  ♡ A J 9 8 4        N                 ♡ 1 0 5 2
  ◇ A 4         W         E            ◇ Q 8 7
  ♣ Q 5 4                S             ♣ K J 9 6 3
                    ♠ K J 8 7 4
                    ♡ 7
                    ◇ K 10 6 5 2
                    ♣ 10 7
```

North has the middle of his range, 16 HCP, but the trumps are good and he's well-prepared for the expected heart lead. With the ◇Q sitting nicely, the hand always makes at least ten tricks.

This is a poster-child hand for the subject of lead-directing doubles, which are grossly overused. If you moved West's ♣Q over to his heart suit that would make it better, but the actual West hand isn't one that should demand a heart lead. With values in the other suits, he is perfectly content whatever partner decides to lead.

West's decision turned out to be a disaster for two reasons. First off, it enabled the opponents to confirm via the 'free' acceptance that they indeed had an eight-card spade fit. Moreover, when East obediently led a heart, dummy's potential club loser eventually went away. He might otherwise have started his long suit, and netted his side an extra trick that would have been crucial at matchpoints.

5)   North-South vul.

♠ J 5 4 2   ♡ A J 7   ◇ A 10 7 6 2   ♣ 7

West	North	East	South
			pass
pass	1♠	pass	?

This would be an ideal hand for a fit-showing jump to 3◇ as a passed hand. If you haven't specifically discussed it, though, rather than sail into uncharted waters, you should content yourself with a Drury 2♣.

Opener rebids 2♠, showing a hand that he isn't especially proud of. This hand has grown up so much with spades as trumps that it's worth a further bid. Now you can complete the picture with 3◇, showing a good supporting hand with a decent side suit. After this you've done your all, and it's up to partner to reconsider the game chances in light of the information you've provided.

How does this scene play out? Well, it's going to hinge on opener's next call, as the hand is:

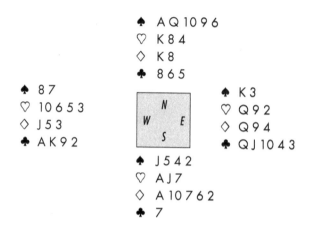

```
                    ♠  A Q 10 9 6
                    ♡  K 8 4
                    ◇  K 8
                    ♣  8 6 5
   ♠  8 7                              ♠  K 3
   ♡  10 6 5 3          N              ♡  Q 9 2
   ◇  J 5 3        W         E         ◇  Q 9 4
   ♣  A K 9 2          S              ♣  Q J 10 4 3
                    ♠  J 5 4 2
                    ♡  A J 7
                    ◇  A 10 7 6 2
                    ♣  7
```

Opener's thoughts should be, 'Well, I've told partner I'm not interested but he's still trying. At least I know my king of diamonds is useful now so I'll play along with 3♡.'

As you can see, responder will gladly bid on to 4♠ now, confident that he'll have the tickets opener needs. The trump finesse loses, but the rest of the news is good and the contract makes with an overtrick.

A friend of mine once remarked that while a passed hand is never entitled to bid game, he can make two moves in that direction. This example is one such case in point, as South doesn't have just a normal invite after the third-seat opening, he has an absolute goldmine. Sometimes Drury is not enough, and responder shouldn't let partner off the hook without making a further effort.

CHAPTER 9

EXTRAS AND REFINEMENTS

A lot of ground has been covered in the first eight chapters, and I believe that once you have a firm grasp of those principles, your results in competitive situations will improve dramatically. You should now be able to function smoothly with partner and hold your own in these tussles without getting pushed around by the opponents.

Of course, there are many more bells and whistles that a partnership can elect to add to their convention card. There are a vast number of ideas that have been suggested in recent years, and even the ones I'll be discussing in this section are just the tip of the iceberg.

To borrow a term from purchasing a vehicle, however, these are luxury options rather than part of the basic package. You'll still have a comfortable ride without them, but you may find the add-ons intriguing and like the dash of spice they offer. They all have some usefulness, but any treatment that you add to the mix has to feel natural and logical rather than a burden on the memory cells. As you read through the list, some of them probably won't have much appeal and you shouldn't give them a second thought. There are others you may take a shine to, and you can make a note of those concepts. You can then have partner browse through them independently and compare your favorites together. In this way, you can discover the ones that have a mutual appeal and perhaps give them a try.

More Defenses to 1NT

We've already had a look at three methods of competing against the opponents' 1NT opening but there are scads more. I'm going to limit myself to two of them. However, as you browse through the various systems, there are several things to keep in mind. All of them have to give up *something*. For example, having the penalty double and natural major-suit overcalls restricts your ability to show two-suited hands. Conversely, a treatment such as DONT will permit you to describe all two-suited hands and play at the cheapest level, but you give up the penalty double and the one-suiters are shown in a roundabout fashion. The bottom line is that there isn't enough space to have it all, so you have to choose what is most essential in your opinion. It's a matter of you and partner getting together to determine what your main priorities are. Then you can select a defense that meets your needs and, just as importantly, won't be forgotten in the heat of battle.

The next issue, which I briefly referred to in Chapter 5, is deciding whether or not to have one system against weak notrumps and another against strong. Some players want to have a penalty double available against lesser notrumps but many pairs are fine with using one defense for all ranges.

Of the many defenses I could present here, I've chosen two because they are simple, and also similar enough that if you want to play one against weak notrumps and the other against strong, it's not too hard.

	Becker (vs. either)	Meckwell (vs. strong)
dbl	penalty	one minor or a major-minor two-suiter
2♣	minors	minors
2◇	majors	majors
2♡	natural	natural
2♠	natural	natural
2NT	minors	minors
3♣	natural	natural

Becker and Meckwell, as you'll note, have two bids to show the minor suits. You can choose one to emphasize high-card strength and the other for more distributional hands. The conventions are identical except for the double, which against strong notrumps becomes the way to show a long minor or a major/minor hand. Partner is asked to bid 2♣, allowing the doubler room to show which hand type he has.

Negative Doubles 301 — Free Bids and the Competitive 2NT

After a negative double, it's commonplace for overcaller's partner to raise whenever he has support, just to make life a bit more difficult for your side. This may pose a challenge for opener in some instances. Back in Chapter 4, when we dealt with the topic of free bids, I suggested that voluntary three-level actions ought to promise extras. Sometimes, however, this approach becomes restrictive if your shape is nice but the high-card values are limited. You'd dearly love to have a way to compete in a manner that denies any real game ambitions, but how?

There is a solution, provided that you and partner are willing to discard 2NT as a natural bid and give it a Lebensohl flavor instead. That gives opener two routes to show his distribution. The direct rebids imply the really good stuff, a bunch of high cards and/or excellent trick-taking ability. However, opener can also contest the auction by bidding 2NT, asking the negative doubler to bid 3♣. He then passes or bids one of the other suits. By proceeding to his objective in a delayed fashion, he is showing 12 to a bad 15 HCP, but a hand worthy of competing to the three-level on the basis of unbalanced distribution.

This convention is named the 'Good-Bad 2NT', and is another invention from the Marty Bergen-Larry Cohen camp. The basis of it is that opener's 2NT is never going to be made on a truly bad hand, just that he might not be bursting at the seams with high cards when he chooses that way of going to the three-level.

At any rate, we can look at some hands and see how it all works, using this auction as our backdrop:

LHO	Partner	RHO	You
			1◇
1♠	dbl	2♣	?

♠6 ♡K73 ◇AKJ10 86 ♣AJ7

Bid 3◇. With 16 HCP and a one-loser suit, make the direct three-level bid to tell partner that you have a juicy hand and that game might be within the realm of possibility.

♠8 ♡A32 ◇KJ9864 ♣KQ10

Here bid 2NT, and then convert to 3◇ when partner bids the obedient 3♣. This is a six-loser hand so it's right to bid, and doing it in this manner tells responder you don't want to try for game.

♠96 ♡AKJ5 ◇K10543 ♣AJ

Bid 3♡. Once again, by heading to your destination right away, you are giving partner some encouragement that there could be a game your way.

♠87 ♡K1086 ◇A9743 ♣AQ

Bid 2NT, followed by 3♡ after responder's 3♣. You have enough to give 3♡ a play, but have no aspirations beyond that. Partner is duly warned that he needs more than just a garden-variety negative double to bid on.

♠J42 ♡A ◇AK1085 ♣KQ93

Bid 3♣, to advertise a two-suiter of fine quality. Game is possible if partner has either shortness or a high card in spades.

♠7 ♡A9 ◇KQ875 ♣Q10743

Bid 2NT, then pass when partner complies with 3♣. The loser count is six, but you have an absolute minimum in terms of point-count, so you don't want partner getting too carried away. The Good-Bad 2NT is the way to compete yet apply a braking mechanism at the same time.

Now let's go over to the other side of the table so we can discuss what the reaction should be to opener's 2NT with the auction having continued:

LHO	Partner	RHO	You
	1◇	1♠	dbl
2♠	2NT*	pass	?

You are being asked to bid 3♣, and will usually do so. However, if you have no wish for that to be the final contract, then you should bid something else. With that in mind, we can move on to the following three hands:

♠J64 ♡A972 ◇85 ♣KJ73

Bid 3♣. You have a typical negative double, so comply with opener's request and let him place the contract.

♠97 ♡AJ98 ◇K532 ♣J76

Bid 3◇. You doubled in the hope of finding a 4-4 heart fit, intending to support diamonds if that didn't pan out. Since opener might be intending to play in 3♣ on the assumption that you have at least four of them, you need to show that you really prefer diamonds as the trump suit.

♠105 ♡QJ10852 ◇J9 ♣A83

Bid 3♡. The purpose of the negative double was to follow up with your hearts, showing your long suit and a minimum-range hand of 6-10 points. There is no reason to deviate from your original plan of action now. Your suit is good enough to play opposite a doubleton if that is all partner has.

OBAR BIDS

What are your thoughts on the auction for this set of hands? Neither side is vulnerable:

LHO	Partner	RHO	You
1♥	pass	2♥	all pass

You ♠ K J 8 4 ♡ 7 ◇ Q 10 5 3 2 ♣ K 9 8

Partner ♠ A 10 7 6 ♡ Q 8 5 4 ◇ K 7 ♣ Q 6 2

The opponents go down one in 2♡, but you find your score is not a good one since a spade contract was often played in your direction, usually making eight or nine tricks for +110 to +140.

What makes the result tough to swallow is that there was no clear blunder made by either player. You were short in hearts but only had 9 HCP. Partner had the points to balance, but not enough support for the minors to reopen with a double.

How, then, did some pairs manage to get into bidding and successfully compete in spades? There are two possibilities. One is that they might have decided to adopt another Marty Bergen treatment that goes by the name of OBAR BIDS. That's an acronym for Opponents Bid And Raise — Balance In Direct Seat.

The theory goes like this: you will double on your 9 HCP after responder's 2♡ as you have the right shape, even with the values being somewhat meager. The logic for what may seem like a rash and foolhardy action is that if 2♡ gets passed around to partner, he'll have too much length in hearts for balancing to be feasible.

Playing OBAR BIDS, the advancer has to pull in his horns somewhat when choosing his bid given that partner can be light for his double. Partner has 11 HCP but only 9 of them are working since the ♡Q rates to be a non-card. Rather than jump to 3♠, he'd have to content himself with 2♠, in accordance with the matchpoint philosophy of not jeopardizing a plus score. Move the ♡Q over to the spade suit and now the hand *is* worth an invitational jump, even in a pre-balancing style.

At least two partnerships landed in 2♠ without direct action by your hand. It was partner who came in with 2♠ on his four-card suit in balancing position. He was mildly fortunate to buy that much support in dummy, but there were reasonable chances of getting at least three of them, as you can't have more than one heart.

What this hand demonstrates is that there are a couple of paths to a good result for your side. If both players are too cautious, though, it isn't going to happen. You can be on one side of the fence and agree to OBAR BIDS in direct seat, in which case you needn't strain to balance unless you have the right hand for it. Alternatively, if you require better hands for the immediate plunge, the person on the other side of the table may have to take some calculated (but not outlandish) risks in balancing.

Support Doubles

A fair number of partnerships deploy this Eric Rodwell invention after an opening bid and a response, with the fourth player then overcalling. An auction of this type would be:

LHO	Partner	RHO	You
	1◇	pass	1♡
1♠	?		

Without discussion, a double by opener is for penalties. However, there won't be that great a frequency of holding a really powerful hand with length in the enemy suit. Consequently, some feel the double is better used for other purposes. One such idea is to have it show precisely three-card support for the major responder has just bid. The strength is variable as opener could have nothing much extra all the way up to a very good hand. This 'support' double merely shows that he has three cards in responder's suit.

The aim of support doubles is for the partnership not to be on a guess as to whether they have an eight-card major-suit fit. Opener needs four to raise, and shows three via the double. Whenever responder has a five-card suit, you have your fit. If he only has four opposite partner's double, he can either choose to play a 4-3 fit, or avoid it, depending on his suit quality.

I've used this convention in some of my partnerships and not in others, so I'm fairly neutral regarding the subject. My only advice is that if you adopt support doubles, opener's hand should look and feel like a raise. To get my drift, look at this set of hands for opener:

LHO	Partner	RHO	You
			1◇
pass	1♡	1♠	?

♠A 4   ♡K J 10   ◇A Q 8 7 6   ♣8 4 3

Yes, by all means go with the support double. You have 14 HCP, three good trumps and a five-card suit as a source of tricks.

♠J65 ♡A54 ◇QJ632 ♣AJ

Double again. This isn't quite as promising a hand as the first one, but if but if you have an agreement, you're best off sticking to it within reason.

♠J83 ♡J62 ◇QJ54 ♣AKJ

Pass. With any convention you are permitted to rely on your judgment. Even the most fervent advocates of the support double wouldn't be overly enthusiastic about making one here. Everything reeks about this 13-count. It's a nine-loser hand that looks more suited to defense than offense. Your holding in their suit is lousy, and the three cards in partner's suit are equally uninspiring.

♠J65 ♡A542 ◇QJ63 ♣AJ

On this hand, make your normal raise to 2♡, but now partner will know you have four of them. That may help later LoTT decision-making.

Unusual versus Unusual When We Open a Major Suit

In Chapter 3, I went into some detail about coping with two-suited overcalls. The sequence I didn't get into was the one where your side opens in a major suit and they bid the Unusual 2NT. That was because the method a lot of players select is fairly intricate, and there are several variations of it. I left it until now, feeling it belonged to this chapter rather than an earlier one.

Unusual versus Unusual relies on the following cornerstones:

- 3NT is to play.
- Double shows 10+ HCP, denies a fit, and should have interest in penalizing one or both of their minor suits.
- Bidding the other major at the three-level is natural and forcing.
- Supporting opener's major at the three-level requires a hand of 8 to a bad 10 points.
- A jump to game in opener's major is just like 1♡ (1♠) 4♡ — less than 10 HCP but great trump support and/or ruffing values.
- That leaves the bids of the minor suits RHO is showing, 3♣ and 3◇. Those will both promise good supporting hands for opener's major. The range for the cheaper of these bids, 3♣, is 10-11 HCP, whereas 3◇ by responder suggests 12+ points and is forcing to game.

With this information in place, we can now look at some hands, with this auction as our launching point.

	LHO	Partner	RHO	You
		1♡	2NT	?

♠K9865 ♡Q104 ◇A96 ♣53

Bid 3♡. You have the upper end of a single raise, so get in the support now as they might freeze you out of the auction if you pass.

♠A754 ♡K1096 ◇42 ♣K87

Bid 3♣. With 10 HCP, four-card support and a doubleton, use the cheaper of their suits to describe a limit raise in hearts.

♠KQ106 ♡A965 ◇AJ4 ♣63

Bid 3◇. The more expensive of the cuebids tells opener that you like his hearts and have sufficient values for game.

♠QJ87 ♡AJ943 ◇5 ♣762

Bid 4♡. This is still a distributional game raise of fewer than 10 HCP.

♠KJ64 ♡QJ73 ◇AQ82 ♣9

Bid 4♣. Overcaller has shown 5-5 in the minors, so both this jump and 4◇ would be splinter raises, with at least four trumps for opener, shortness in the bid suit and enough points for game. If you catch partner with a better-than-minimum hand, slam is definitely possible.

♠AJ10543 ♡K8 ◇75 ♣KQ6

Bid 3♠. New suits at the three-level force to game. With luck, opener has support, but you will have a useful dummy even if he repeats the hearts or bids 3NT.

♠KJ8652 ♡Q ◇K84 ♣962

Pass. You'd like to introduce the spades, but the values aren't quite there to do it. It would be forcing, and if partner can't support your suit, you might not have a port in the impending storm. Perhaps they'll settle in a minor suit and then you can bid a delayed 3♠, after which partner should get the message that you aren't that strong.

$\spadesuit$ A K 1 0 6 2 $\heartsuit$ 6 4 $\diamondsuit$ K J 9 7 $\clubsuit$ Q 5

Double. You could bid 3$\spadesuit$, but that can wait. With three likely diamond tricks behind the 2NT bidder, you could be in business if partner has clubs. If LHO bids 3$\clubsuit$ and partner can't take a piece of it, you can then mention the spades — now, because you doubled to show 10+ points and then bid a new suit, the auction would be forcing.

REVISED UNUSUAL VERSUS UNUSUAL

There are actually several improved versions of Unusual versus Unusual, but I'll confine myself to one of them. The main differences are:

- Version two uses 3$\clubsuit$ to show all good supporting hands. It is a limit raise *or better* in opener's major, and if responder has 12+ he will carry on to game even if opener signs off.
- 3$\diamondsuit$ now shows the other major and the values to compete but not enough to force game. Responder can now use that bid for the second-last of our example hands, where he has the long spades.

Leaping Michaels

The next convention is designed primarily for occasions where the opponents open a weak two-bid. Let's say your RHO opens 2$\spadesuit$, and try to determine the priorities.

The first order of business is to decide what a 3$\spadesuit$ cuebid should be. There are two options. One could be that you have a super hand that can play 3NT if partner has a stopper, such as:

$\spadesuit$ 6 $\heartsuit$ A Q $\diamondsuit$ A K Q 10 8 5 3 $\clubsuit$ K 9 8

However, that leaves you in a somewhat of a pickle if you have:

$\spadesuit$ 7 $\heartsuit$ A K Q 9 4 $\diamondsuit$ A Q 10 6 5 3 $\clubsuit$ 8

And that is why some pairs opt for a Michaels treatment on the cuebid, to show hearts and one of the minors. But now you have to be on the same wavelength as partner on how to proceed. There is no longer a convenient 2NT bid available to ask for overcaller's minor. Is 3NT to play or asking which minor you have? Or should 4$\clubsuit$ be the enquiry instead? Moreover, if LHO rockets into 4$\spadesuit$, partner will have to brave the five-level to play in your minor suit if he doesn't have hearts.

While you're grappling for a way to show each of these hands, ask yourself this: have you ever in your life jumped to 4♣ or 4◇ when they open a weak-two in either major? If the answer is no, or just once in a blue moon, let me introduce you to the world of Leaping Michaels.

The auction that serves as our lead-in is:

LHO	Partner	RHO	You
		2♠	?

This is how you can embrace both of the hand types shown above:

- The direct cuebid, 3♠, is looking for 3NT and asks partner to bid it if he has a stopper in the enemy suit. Partner doesn't have to worry about what he has in the other suits. If he can stop the opponents from running spades, 3NT should be the only thought that enters his head. Otherwise, he'll make the cheapest bid, 4♣, so that you can play in whatever your long suit is.
- A *jump* to four of a minor shows the bid minor and the other major, hearts in this case. To make this bid, you need a hand where you can take at least nine tricks on your own and a single useful card from partner should be enough for game. The second of our example hands would be good enough for a LM jump to 4◇.

Leaping Michaels hasn't gained universal acceptance as of yet, but is becoming increasingly well known. Quite by accident, my wife and I discovered a similar situation where the idea could be used, while playing in America's largest Regional in Gatlinburg, Tennessee. The auction went:

LHO	Me	RHO	Sue
		1♠	pass
2♠	4♣	pass	?

I had ten cards in hearts and clubs, and a three-loser hand. We hadn't discussed it, but I figured I'd throw out 4♣ to see if she'd read it as a Leaping Michaels scenario. Sue refers to these forays of mine as 'wonder bids' in a scathing tone of voice. She blinked and cursed at me silently, but eventually shrugged and bid 4♡, having decided that was the only thing it could be. I subsequently mentioned the hand to some of the top players at the event. They had never thought of using the convention in these auctions, but agreed that it made perfect sense to do so.

QUIZ HANDS

1) You're looking at these cards, vulnerable against not:

♠ 8 7 4   ♡ A J 10 4   ◇ K 5   ♣ K 10 9 7

The bidding proceeds:

West	North	East	South
pass	1◇	1♠	dbl
2♠	3♣	pass	?

Your side might just be able to buy the contract. Is there any reason to look for anything more?

2) Things are looking black as you sort out the cards for the next hand:

♠ A K J 4 2   ♡ 7   ◇ 4   ♣ K Q J 8 7 3

Your side is vulnerable, they are not. You can forget about taking your sweet time to describe this hand, as the opponents have bid and raised before you get your chance:

West	North	East	South
1♡	pass	2♡	?

The challenge now is how to show both the distribution and trick-taking ability of this hand. What course of bidding leaves you in the most advantageous position?

3) Neither side vulnerable, you get dealt more than your share of the points:

♠ 9 4 2   ♡ A Q 6 5   ◇ Q 10 4   ♣ A 7 3

West	North	East	South
1♠	pass	2♠	?

You have 12 points and four-card support for the unbid major. Do you pre-balance in direct seat, knowing that partner might not have the hand for it if you pass it around to him?

4) Vulnerable against not, the hand you've just been dealt hardly brings a grin to your face:

♠KJ932 ♡J542 ◇Q4 ♣65

The good news is that for once, your side gets to bid first. Naturally, since this book is all about competitive bidding, you won't be getting a free run:

West	North	East	South
	1◇	pass	1♠
2♣	dbl*	3♣	?

Opener has made a support double, promising three of your spades. You were going to retreat to 2♠, but RHO has now gone to 3♣. Should you keep on trucking to the three-level or not with this hand?

1)   North-South vul.

♠ 8 7 4   ♡ A J 10 4   ◇ K 5   ♣ K 10 9 7

The bidding proceeds:

West	North	East	South
pass	1◇	1♠	dbl
2♠	3♣	pass	?

Opener has bid voluntarily over LHO's raise, so he should be at least a king more than a bare minimum. On top of that, the auction so far suggests that he doesn't have many spades, two at most and perhaps even a singleton.

Your hand, meanwhile has improved considerably with his second bid. You have no wastage in spades, the ♡A, and best of all, the king in each of partner's long suits. You should be thinking in terms of game, the only question being whether to look for 3NT or to go directly to 5♣.

When partner sees what you have for him, he'll be quite happy, as the full deal is:

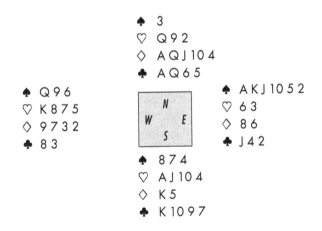

```
                  ♠ 3
                  ♡ Q 9 2
                  ◇ A Q J 10 4
                  ♣ A Q 6 5
  ♠ Q 9 6                      ♠ A K J 10 5 2
  ♡ K 8 7 5         N          ♡ 6 3
  ◇ 9 7 3 2     W       E      ◇ 8 6
  ♣ 8 3             S          ♣ J 4 2
                  ♠ 8 7 4
                  ♡ A J 10 4
                  ◇ K 5
                  ♣ K 10 9 7
```

Making 5♣ presents no difficulty as declarer ruffs the second spade, draws trumps, takes discards on his long diamonds and has the heart finesse for a potential overtrick.

Is West's hand good enough to bid 2♠ over the negative double? With a ruffing value and the hope that the ♡K is a trick, it's definitely enterprising but not ludicrous.

Suppose we relieve North of the ♢Q, changing the hand to:

♠ 3   ♡ Q 9 2   ♢ A J 10 8 4   ♣ A Q 6 5

He is no longer worth a 3♣ bid, but if the partnership had agreed to play the Good-Bad 2NT, he could then use that to ask you to bid 3♣ and show enough distribution to compete without a wealth of high cards.

What if you hadn't adopted the Good-Bad 2NT? Would the opponents have stolen the hand in 2♠? Not at all, because with an 11-count, you can make a second double and opener will then bid clubs, so you'll still get to the right spot.

2)   North-South vul.

♠ A K J 4 2   ♡ 7   ♢ 4   ♣ K Q J 8 7 3

West	North	East	South
1♡	pass	2♡	?

If you and partner have discussed and bought into the Leaping Michaels concept, you'll have no problem at all in showing the nature of your hand. A jump to 4♣ will describe a hand with 5-5 or better in clubs and spades along with the capability of taking nine or ten tricks with one of those suits as trumps.

If you don't have that option at your disposal, there are two ways to go on this hand:

- Bid 3♡, which partner will likely take as regular Michaels. In the event that the opponents go on to 4♡ and partner can't bid 4♠, you're going to have to introduce your clubs at the five-level.
- Bid 3♣ instead. Yes, it does leave the spades temporarily out of the picture, but you're hoping one of the opponents will persist in hearts. Your next salvo will be 4♠, and partner will at least be able to select one of your suits at the four-level. As Al Roth used to say, 'Well placed if the auction continues.'

In fact, this is one of those hands where both sides will keep on bidding for a while:

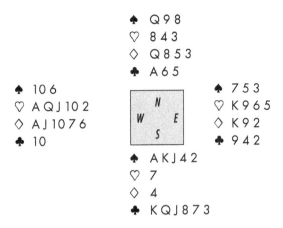

```
                    ♠  Q 9 8
                    ♡  8 4 3
                    ◊  Q 8 5 3
                    ♣  A 6 5
    ♠  10 6                          ♠  7 5 3
    ♡  A Q J 10 2        N           ♡  K 9 6 5
    ◊  A J 10 7 6    W       E       ◊  K 9 2
    ♣  10               S           ♣  9 4 2
                    ♠  A K J 4 2
                    ♡  7
                    ◊  4
                    ♣  K Q J 8 7 3
```

Regardless of how the bidding goes, West won't sell out to 4♠ or 5♣, and will continue on to 5♡. It's a worthwhile sacrifice as it fails by only one or two tricks, depending on how he plays the diamond suit. North-South are cold for eleven tricks in either black suit. If South gets in both the clubs and spades in time, North should forge on as he has two valuable cards in the ♠Q and ♣A. A Leaping Michaels bid of 4♣, if you have it in your toolbox, is a definite winner as North will know precisely which suits and how many tricks you'll have. There will be no doubt in his mind that your side will be gin for 5♠ if you have the nine or ten tricks that you've promised.

3) Neither vul.

♠ 9 4 2   ♡ A Q 6 5   ◊ Q 10 4   ♣ A 7 3

West	North	East	South
1♣	pass	2♣	?

The aspects of this hand that favor entering the fray with a double are the 12 HCP and four-card heart support. However, it doesn't afford enough distributional security. With your 4333 shape, the likelihood of an eight-card fit is somewhat reduced. In these close decisions, it's a good idea to let the overall texture of your hand and the quality of your spot cards act as a tie-breaker. Here again, the picture isn't that bright as you have one lonely ten-spot and your queens are lying under the opening bidder. Although it's somewhat tempting, there isn't enough to recommend sticking your neck out on these cards. Granted, it might work on occasion, but more often than not, you're likely to get burnt, particularly against opponents who know how to pull out the red card.

In fact, this deal is one in which you won't be getting off lightly if you take action:

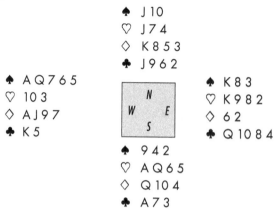

```
                          ♠ J 10
                          ♡ J 7 4
                          ◇ K 8 5 3
                          ♣ J 9 6 2
    ♠ A Q 7 6 5                              ♠ K 8 3
    ♡ 10 3                    N              ♡ K 9 8 2
    ◇ A J 9 7           W          E         ◇ 6 2
    ♣ K 5                      S              ♣ Q 10 8 4
                          ♠ 9 4 2
                          ♡ A Q 6 5
                          ◇ Q 10 4
                          ♣ A 7 3
```

Alas, partner doesn't have four hearts or a five-card minor. Worse yet, the opponents will surely double since East can take care of hearts and clubs while opener can handle any attempt to settle in a diamond contract.

Your queens do turn out to be of some use with the heart finesse winning and partner having the ◇K. The lack of spot cards hurts, though, as you can't avoid two losers each in diamonds and clubs.

The division of the remaining high-card points should come as no surprise. Since many players nowadays use 2/1 with forcing notrump responses, the single raise by RHO is typically constructive, showing a good 7 to 9 HCP. That is why the proper distribution is very important to have if you choose to wade in. Exchange a spade for an extra minor-suit card, giving South one of these hands:

♠ 4 2 ♡ A Q 6 5 ◇ Q 10 7 4 ♣ A 7 3

♠ 4 2 ♡ A Q 6 5 ◇ Q 10 4 ♣ A 7 5 3

and now a double by South would result in a gain more often than not.

One side point of interest on this hand is what North should do once partner makes a takeout double. We've already seen that a bid of 2NT in competition is not always natural and to play. Similarly, in auctions like this, many pairs choose to use 2NT by advancer as showing equal length in the minors and asking the doubler to pick between clubs and diamonds. That will ensure our side getting to a 4-4 fit rather than having to struggle in a contract that has just seven trumps between us.

4)　　North-South vul.

♠ K J 9 3 2　♡ J 5 4 2　◇ Q 4　♣ 6 5

West	North	East	South
	1◇	pass	1♠
2♣	dbl*	3♣	?

You know from partner's support double that he has three of your spades, and you were about to bid 2♠ until RHO made a nuisance of himself with the 3♣ raise. Does this hand justify taking the push to the three-level in our eight-card fit?

It has 5-4 shape and the queen of partner's suit may be useful, but it's still a minimum. You have potential heart losers and the opponents could lead trumps to deprive you of the ability to ruff them in dummy. My preference would be to pass, but more intrepid souls would persist with 3♠.

In the end, it doesn't matter whether you bid on or not, as opener isn't yet finished:

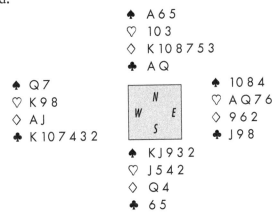

```
          ♠  A 6 5
          ♡  10 3
          ◇  K 10 8 7 5 3
          ♣  A Q
♠ Q 7                        ♠  10 8 4
♡ K 9 8          N           ♡  A Q 7 6
◇ A J        W       E       ◇  9 6 2
♣ K 10 7 4 3 2       S       ♣  J 9 8
          ♠  K J 9 3 2
          ♡  J 5 4 2
          ◇  Q 4
          ♣  6 5
```

Opener will now bid 3◇, showing six of them, and you'll most likely go back to 3♠. By playing to establish the diamonds right off the bat, declarer should come home with nine tricks.

The support double is good to have from opener's perspective on this hand. Instead of repeating the diamonds and then having to guess whether to show his three spades later on, he can advertise the support with the double *first* and then compete in diamonds, ensuring his side will get to their best fit.

CHAPTER 10

FINAL QUIZ

In the preceding nine chapters, a lot of ground has been covered. We've learned, with the help of examples from actual play, how you can gain handsomely from competing aggressively if you have good suits and unbalanced hands. Our journey began with the five cornerstones of competitive bidding: overcalls, takeout and negative doubles, preempts and two-suited overcalls. The horizons were widened over the next four chapters as sandwich actions, balancing, notrump auctions and free bids were brought into the picture along with low- and high-level bidding decisions. Chapter 8 focused on partnership discussion and agreements, and Chapter 9 described some of the fancier competitive treatments that are out there in the present-day environment.

To wind up, I'll present a final ten-question quiz. The majority of the questions deal with themes that have made an appearance at some time during the book. A few break new ground, but even so, logic should guide you to the proper action to take. After all, it's impossible to have discussed every possible auction with your partner — there will be times when you just have to apply basic principles and wing it.

Here goes!

1) You are vulnerable against not, gazing at these cards:

♠106542　♡AQ5　◇J97　♣Q3

The bidding story has unfolded thus:

West	North	East	South
	1♣	pass	1♠
2♡	3♣	pass	?

You don't have the moon and the stars pointwise. So is that all she wrote or is there a reason to continue on?

2) For this one, with both sides vulnerable, you hold:

♠A65 ♡AQ954 ◇62 ♣962

Everyone is in the auction when it comes your turn to bid:

West	North	East	South
1◇	1♠	dbl	?

You certainly have enough to make a statement of your own with your high cards and an adequate fit. What's the best way to describe the hand?

3) For the next challenge, with neither side vulnerable, you have:

♠A763 ♡7 ◇AK62 ♣AKQ4

You're looking forward to opening a minor and then showing your unbalanced powerhouse when your cohort tosses his hat into the ring first:

West	North	East	South
pass	2♡	pass	?

So... even though partner is showing six hearts and less than opening values, you aren't so easily deterred. That said, what route are you going to proceed along and what destination should you have in mind?

4) And now your side is vulnerable and they are not:

♠AQ107 ♡Q7 ◇8732 ♣A43

As you toy with the idea of opening, RHO steps up to the plate first:

West	North	East	South
		1♡	?

With decent points and respectable support for the unbid suits, do you get involved at this point? What is your inclination?

5) With neither side vulnerable, you are dealt these cards:

♠A9 ♡KJ9742 ◇A64 ♣74

Having the chance to bid first as dealer, you open 1♡. Partner makes a 2/1 response, but RHO just can't leave well enough alone and makes his presence felt:

West	North	East	South
			1♡
pass	2♣	2♠	?

So much for your easy 2♡ rebid. What to do now?

6) Both vulnerable, you pick up this very average-looking hand:

♠10854 ♡K108 ◇KJ85 ♣K6

Of course, you get left by the wayside as all the other players at the table have their say:

West	North	East	South
		1◇	pass
1NT	dbl	pass	?

How do you interpret partner's double? And more to the point, how do you react to it?

7) They are vulnerable, you're not and you get dealt this threadbare collection:

♠K98732 ♡1087 ◇4 ♣J108

It seems to be your day for having good support, however, as the bidding commences with:

West	North	East	South
1◇	1♠	dbl	?

How vigorously should you raise partner?

8) Both vulnerable, and the hands are getting wilder now:

♠9 3 ♡— ◇K Q J 8 5 4 ♣10 9 6 3 2

Partner at least opens a suit that you like:

West	North	East	South
	1♣	1♠	?

With another super fit, what's the best effort for your side? You and partner have decided to include fit-showing jumps in your toolkit.

9) For your next competitive excursion, you're vulnerable against not, with sound opening values:

♠6 ♡K 10 8 4 2 ◇A 8 3 ♣K Q 9 6

Naturally, they open but you're able to overcall conveniently:

West	North	East	South
	pass	1◇	1♡
dbl	1♠	2◇	?

Everyone seems to have an opinion in the bidding. Should you venture any further action at this juncture?

10) For the last hurrah, neither side is vulnerable:

♠K 10 6 5 ♡7 6 ◇K 9 7 6 4 ♣9 3

It turns out to be a hand where the opponents in this day and age won't let you play 1NT, and you are faced with the eternal question of whether to defend or bid:

West	North	East	South
pass	1NT	pass	pass
2♡	pass	pass	?

1)   North-South vul.

♠ 106542   ♡ A Q 5   ◊ J 9 7   ♣ Q 3

West	North	East	South
	1♣	pass	1♠
2♡	3♣	pass	?

As I mentioned in Chapter 4, a free bid at the three-level has to show better than a minimum hand. Opener should therefore have 15+ HCP or good shape with at most six losers. That being the case, your hand has sufficient potential to try 3NT, as the clubs should run and you have a double heart stopper.

Does the push to game yield dividends for your side? Here's the layout of the hand:

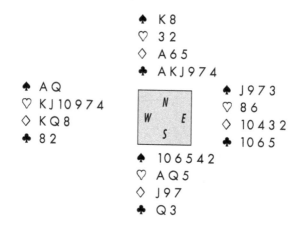

```
              ♠  K 8
              ♡  3 2
              ◊  A 6 5
              ♣  A K J 9 7 4
 ♠ A Q                        ♠  J 9 7 3
 ♡ K J 10 9 7 4        N      ♡  8 6
 ◊ K Q 8           W       E  ◊  10 4 3 2
 ♣ 8 2                 S      ♣  10 6 5
              ♠  10 6 5 4 2
              ♡  A Q 5
              ◊  J 9 7
              ♣  Q 3
```

North has the assets to justify his three-level foray with 15 HCP, six good clubs and a six-loser hand. A heart lead gives you nine tricks right away. Even if West finds the best lead of a neutral club, you can lead up to the ♠K and rake in your game-going trick that way.

2)   Both vul.

♠ A 6 5   ♡ A Q 9 5 4   ◇ 6 2   ♣ 9 6 2

West	North	East	South
1◇	1♠	dbl	?

You could just raise to 2♠, but that would be too conservative. With three-card support and a good five-card suit, you should treat this hand as a limit raise and cuebid 2◇. It's a nice hand for both offense and defense, and by going with the more encouraging raise, you supply overcaller with the information to make the winning choice if their side bids on.

What is the end result on the deal? It will depend on whether the opponents are in a frisky mood or not:

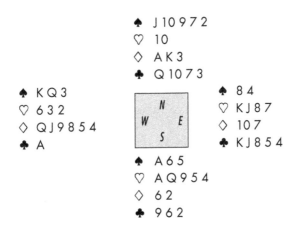

```
                    ♠  J 10 9 7 2
                    ♡  10
                    ◇  A K 3
                    ♣  Q 10 7 3
  ♠ K Q 3                              ♠ 8 4
  ♡ 6 3 2            N                 ♡ K J 8 7
  ◇ Q J 9 8 5 4   W     E             ◇ 10 7
  ♣ A                S                 ♣ K J 8 5 4
                    ♠  A 6 5
                    ♡  A Q 9 5 4
                    ◇  6 2
                    ♣  9 6 2
```

North's hand for his 1♠ bid isn't a thing of beauty but he does have unbalanced distribution and a seven-loser hand, so it suffices for a one-level overcall. Over your 2◇, he will sign off in 2♠, and can scramble home with eight tricks, losing three clubs and two spades.

Note how your side benefits from the strength-showing 2◇ cuebid if West now bids 3◇. North can now double, having the ace, king of trumps and a singleton to lead and expecting a couple of tricks from you. You'll get two hearts, a spade, two diamonds and a heart ruff for +500 as the price they'd pay if they tried to buy the hand.

3)   Neither vul.

♠A763 ♡7 ◇AK62 ♣AKQ4

West	North	East	South
pass	2♡	pass	?

While it's tempting to bid 3NT on these cards, that might not be such a good idea. Ask yourself this: how many of partner's six hearts are going to be tricks in a notrump contract if they aren't solid? Not many, as you'll need a way to get to the table even if you establish the suit, and there might not be a high card to reach dummy with.

Now think about your losers in 4♡. You can afford two or three trump losers and still have a fair shot of bringing the contract home. When bidding opposite a preempt, the high-card points aren't as relevant as the number of sure tricks you have for partner, and here you have an ample quantity of those.

Since 2NT is always an inquiry, whether you're playing the Feature Ask or Ogust, you can try that to see whether the weak two-bidder has anything on the side. If he does, then 3NT might be a possibility, but otherwise you should avoid it like the plague as the six or seven tricks in your hand won't be enough for it to succeed.

Is the actual picture of the entire deal similar to the one we have in our minds? Take a look:

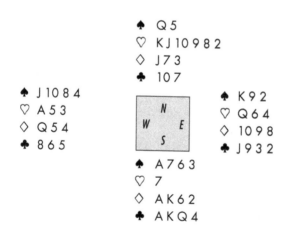

```
              ♠ Q5
              ♡ KJ10982
              ◇ J73
              ♣ 107
♠ J1084                      ♠ K92
♡ A53           N            ♡ Q64
◇ Q54       W       E        ◇ 1098
♣ 865           S            ♣ J932
              ♠ A763
              ♡ 7
              ◇ AK62
              ♣ AKQ4
```

As you can see, North's long suit will only be useful in a heart contract. Meanwhile, 3NT by South is promptly scuttled on the ♠J lead, after which declarer is limited to seven or eight tricks. However, 4♡ will make, losing only two hearts and maybe one other trick.

Depending on system, here is how the partnership can arrive at 4♡:

FEATURE ASK			OGUST	
North	**South**		**North**	**South**
2♡	2NT*		2♡	2NT*
3♡	4♡		3◇*	4♡

In the Feature Ask sequence, North denies an outside ace or king or a solid heart suit, so responder gives up on 3NT and hopes his values are enough for 4♡ to fetch.

In the Ogust auction, North shows a bad hand and a good suit (only because of the excellent spots). South can bid 4♡ with confidence as there shouldn't be more than two tricks to give up in the trump suit.

4)   North-South vul.

♠ A Q 10 7 ♡ Q 7 ◇ 8 7 3 2 ♣ A 4 3

West	North	East	South
		1♡	?

Most bridge players have heard of Eddie Kantar, whose considerable fame as a player is matched or exceeded by his contributions as an author and teacher of the game. In his series of bridge lessons, he makes a great suggestion about takeout doubles with regard to unsupported queens and jacks in opener's suit. His recommendation is that they should be ignored in counting the points in your hand, as they don't rate to be very useful cards. If you follow his advice, this hand dwindles from 12 HCP to only 10 working points, and that isn't enough for a direct-seat action.

The player at the table holding these cards waded in with a takeout double, and the result was less than pleasing for his side:

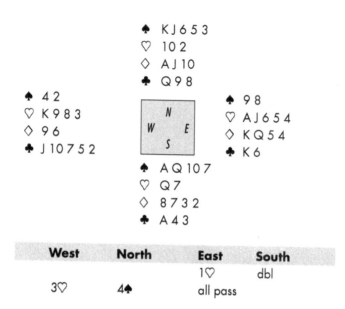

	♠ KJ653		
	♡ 10 2		
	◇ A J 10		
	♣ Q 9 8		

♠ 4 2		♠ 9 8
♡ K 9 8 3		♡ A J 6 5 4
◇ 9 6		◇ K Q 5 4
♣ J 10 7 5 2		♣ K 6

	♠ A Q 10 7
	♡ Q 7
	◇ 8 7 3 2
	♣ A 4 3

West	North	East	South
		1♡	dbl
3♡	4♠	all pass	

After West's preemptive 3♡ raise, North bid 4♠, expecting to have a good play for game opposite even a minimum takeout double, but failed by two tricks. He wasn't too thrilled that partner had included the ♡Q in the valuation of his hand as it proved to be a worthless card. If South passes, his side can enter the auction later regardless of what West does, and manage to stop lower for a better score.

5)   Neither vul.

♠A9 ♡KJ9742 ◇A64 ♣74

West	North	East	South
			1♡
pass	2♣	2♠	?

Should you repeat the hearts anyway, even at a higher level? Remember that in a 2/1 environment, you have the luxury of biding your time and finding out what partner has to say. Bidding 3♡ here would be an emphatic vote for hearts being the trump suit, promising both extra length and outstanding quality in the suit. Your hearts are decent but not glittering, and because of that it seems right to pass and find out what partner has to say. If he bids, you can then repeat the hearts to show more than five of them.

As it turns out, he doubles. Is now the time to pipe in with the heart suit again? You could, but let's try and assess the defensive prospects of the hand. You have two tricks for sure with the aces, possibly a heart trick and maybe even a club ruff. Neither you nor responder is exactly thrilled with each other's suit. You might have a reasonable chance of inflicting some damage on 2♠.

What is the outcome if you elect to sit for the double of 2♠? Pretty good for your side:

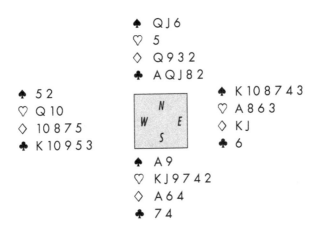

```
                    ♠ Q J 6
                    ♡ 5
                    ♢ Q 9 3 2
                    ♣ A Q J 8 2
    ♠ 5 2                          ♠ K 10 8 7 4 3
    ♡ Q 10          N              ♡ A 8 6 3
    ♢ 10 8 7 5    W   E            ♢ K J
    ♣ K 10 9 5 3     S             ♣ 6
                    ♠ A 9
                    ♡ K J 9 7 4 2
                    ♢ A 6 4
                    ♣ 7 4
```

It turns out that 2♣ doubled is not fun for East. The defense will begin with a club lead and fire a heart back. It matters not what line of play declarer takes, he's in a world of trouble. Down two or three is the normal result, and because any North-South game is doomed to failure, you'll be quite happy with your score.

If you succumb to the urge to rebid hearts, your plus evaporates into a minus.

As an aside, even with his unbalanced hand, East's choice to step into a 2/1 auction was somewhat dubious. West wasn't a favorite to have much assistance and those long hearts were bound to get overruffed by RHO.

6)   Both vul.

♠ 10 8 5 4   ♡ K 10 8   ♢ K J 8 5   ♣ K 6

West	North	East	South
		1♢	pass
1NT	dbl	pass	?

What is partner's double? Going back to Chapter 1, it's a takeout of diamonds, the only suit the opponents have bid, since your side hasn't yet bid and their contract is a partscore.

With your four spades, should you go ahead and mention them? That's reasonable, but first let's consider 1NT, the contract they're in at the moment. With an opening bid and response in front of him, partner should have the goods for his call, so assume 11-13 HCP in his hand. That gives your side an edge of a few points and moreover, the cards don't appear to be sitting very nicely for them. You've got RHO's diamonds and partner will have clubs, the only suit responder can be long in. You can stand the lead of either major, so why not see how they're going to fare in 1NT doubled?

The answer is quite miserably, as we can see by viewing all four hands:

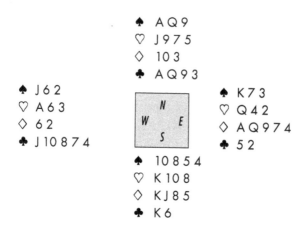

On a heart lead by North, declarer may be held to three or four tricks, a ringing slap in the face to take on such an innocuous-looking deal. There were no major gaffes committed by any of the players. True, some might not approve of East's 1◊, but others would consider it perfectly normal. The key here was for South to recognize that he could possibly reap a windfall by defending instead of bidding once partner made the takeout double.

7)   East-West vul.

♠ K 9 8 7 3 2   ♡ 10 8 7   ◊ 4   ♣ J 10 8

West	North	East	South
1◊	1♠	dbl	?

There is a wonderful fit for partner, but you also have the key component of shortness in the enemy suit. Because of this, a vigorous raise is an appealing option. But how far should you go?

To determine the answer, let us again visualize each side's trick-taking ability. For you, we'll assume between nine and eleven tricks based primarily on your abundance of trumps. What is the prognosis for East-West? You have zippo on defense, and partner's typical overcall will be one to three tricks, so average it out to two.

One of the secrets to effective preemptive bidding is to take your adversaries out of their comfort zone. You could bid 4♠, sure, but one of them will bid on and the calculation we've done indicates they can make eleven tricks in their best spot. Bidding 5♠, on the other hand, is a horse of a different color. It puts them in the gray area where they don't necessarily have a plus in bidding on, and it also tells partner you have a bunch of spades and likely shortness, but no defense to speak of. If there is any further action from them, he'll have the information at his fingertips to do the right thing for our side.

Does the Braveheart jump to 5♠ lead to a good result? Yes it does, if you maintain partnership discipline afterwards:

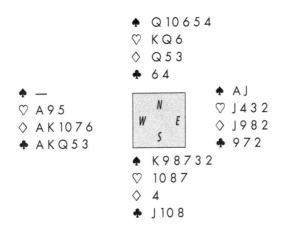

```
                    ♠ Q 10 6 5 4
                    ♡ K Q 6
                    ◇ Q 5 3
                    ♣ 6 4
♠ —                                      ♠ A J
♡ A 9 5            N                      ♡ J 4 3 2
◇ A K 10 7 6    W      E                  ◇ J 9 8 2
♣ A K Q 5 3        S                      ♣ 9 7 2
                    ♠ K 9 8 7 3 2
                    ♡ 10 8 7
                    ◇ 4
                    ♣ J 10 8
```

When this deal occurred at the table, the actual bidding was:

West	North	East	South
1◇	1♠	dbl	5♠
6♣	pass	6◇	6♠
pass	pass	dbl	

West passed 6♠ because he thought a grand slam might still be possible and had first-round spade control. East had no such ambitions and doubled at his turn.

South did a great thing when he rocketed to 5♠, pushing the opponents into a 6◇ contract that was about to go down. Unfortunately, he then took the premature sacrifice without allowing overcaller any kind of input in the decision. Had he passed, North would have done likewise, figuring to get two red-suit tricks from his heart and diamond holdings.

8)   Both vul.

♠ 9 3   ♡ —   ◇ K Q J 8 5 4   ♣ 10 9 6 3 2

West	North	East	South
1♣	1♠	?	

This might seem like a good hand for a fit-showing jump, but it isn't. The convention is always a double-edged sword, because the information you give to partner can also be used by the opponents to their advantage. It functions best when your trump agreement is in a major suit, when you have legitimate expectations of winning the declarership.

This is a situation in which responder should muddy the waters as quickly as possible without revealing the exact nature of his hand, since that information is liable to benefit the opponents more than his side. They will have at least one nine-card fit in a major suit and the objective is to prevent any low-level communication between them. A FSJ of 3◇ won't accomplish that, but a direct bash into 5♣ will. We can now look at the full deal to see what happens:

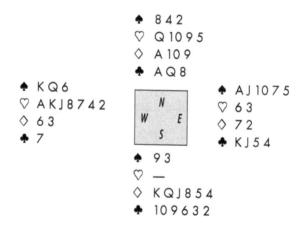

```
              ♠ 8 4 2
              ♡ Q 10 9 5
              ◇ A 10 9
              ♣ A Q 8
♠ K Q 6                      ♠ A J 10 7 5
♡ A K J 8 7 4 2    N         ♡ 6 3
◇ 6 3          W       E     ◇ 7 2
♣ 7                   S      ♣ K J 5 4
              ♠ 9 3
              ♡ —
              ◇ K Q J 8 5 4
              ♣ 10 9 6 3 2
```

If South tries the fit-showing jump of 3◇, West will either jump to 4♡ or cuebid 4♣. If either of you then bids 5♣, West can pass as he's already had the opportunity to describe his hand. East will then wield the axe, as his hand is mostly defense.

Compare that result to West's situation over a jump to 5♣. Since he's not blessed with X-ray vision, he'll certainly bid either 5♡ or 5♠, and now the plus score will be in your column rather than theirs. I held the South cards and the auction continued like this:

West	North	East	South
	1♣	1♠	5♣
5♡	dbl	pass	pass
5♠	dbl	all pass	

Five of either major goes down three, so North-South can notch up +800 their way.

9)   North-South vul.

♠ 6   ♡ K 10 8 4 2   ◇ A 8 3   ♣ K Q 9 6

West	North	East	South
	pass	1◇	1♡
dbl	1♠	2◇	?

As you gain experience in competitive bidding sequences, you'll face certain auctions that should have warning bells going off in your head. This is one of them. By your second turn, the prospects of a fit your way are rapidly dimming. Partner hasn't supported your hearts, and you're not at all enthusiastic about his spades. So the question now is, are you really willing to bet the farm and go to the three-level to see whether he has some clubs with you? Because if he doesn't, the opponents will be letting you know the bad news with a red card.

Aside from that, it's not a matter of supreme importance to play the hand, as you could do as well or better on defense. You have a singleton to lead and the ace of trumps to get in with. That doesn't even include the high cards in clubs and hearts. It wouldn't be a huge surprise to get four or five tricks just from your hand against their 2◇ contract, and partner will have a little something as well.

Passing is the most sensible option with this hand. Double could also turn out to be a winner if the opponents don't have an adequate fit. A 3♣ foray needs partner to have four of them for it to be successful, and is a low-percentage bid when measured up against the other two choices.

We can now lift the curtain on the full deal and find out what awaits:

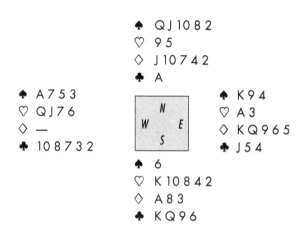

♠ Q J 10 8 2
♡ 9 5
◇ J 10 7 4 2
♣ A

♠ A 7 5 3
♡ Q J 7 6
◇ —
♣ 10 8 7 3 2

♠ K 9 4
♡ A 3
◇ K Q 9 6 5
♣ J 5 4

♠ 6
♡ K 10 8 4 2
◇ A 8 3
♣ K Q 9 6

At the table, the auction went as follows:

West	North	East	South
	pass	1◇	1♡
dbl	1♠	2◇	3♣
dbl	3♡	pass	pass
dbl	all pass		

The bidding resembled a ping-pong match, with lots of questionable actions. To begin with, West's negative double is iffy. Yes, he has support for the unbid suits, but he also has minimum values with wasted heart cards. Another drawback is the void in partner's suit, as he isn't going to be a very happy camper if opener rebids diamonds.

North's 1♠ is acceptable only because of the good spots in the suit, as he's bidding with the knowledge of there being four spades on his right.

East's 2◇ is asking for trouble. Look at it this way: he is expecting four spades and four clubs from responder, who could also have three or four hearts as the overcall hasn't been raised. Crunching those numbers together, it's impossible for him to have enough support for diamonds.

Finally, we have South's 3♣ bid, which is too optimistic a position to take as there is nothing from the previous bidding to indicate that it will strike gold. Now the doubling started, and the resulting 3♡ contract went for -800.

Throughout the auction, there were indicators from every bid made that danger was lurking for both sides. All parties at the table were guilty of tuning out those messages and once South went over the brink to the three-level, he ran out of second chances.

10)   Neither vul.

♠ K 10 6 5   ♡ 7 6   ◇ K 9 7 6 4   ♣ 9 3

West	North	East	South
pass	1NT	pass	pass
2♡	pass	pass	?

With partner's strong notrump opening, you have over half the points in the deck, and because of your 5-4 shape, it doesn't seem right to let them have it for 2♡.

It seems obvious to bid the diamonds, but thanks to your initial pass, you have a more flexible bid if partner reads it correctly. What you can do now is bid 2♠. Opener will be scratching his head and wondering what this is all about. The conclusion he should arrive at is that you only have four spades, as you didn't transfer. Since mentioning a four-card suit is not very typical or all that safe, he'll surmise that you have another suit to play in if he doesn't care for your spades.

How do you fare in your experiment in looking for the best destination for your side? Very well, as it turns out:

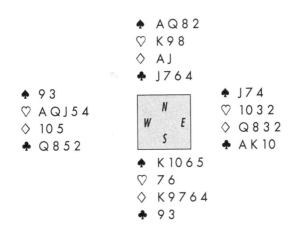

```
              ♠ A Q 8 2
              ♡ K 9 8
              ◇ A J
              ♣ J 7 6 4
 ♠ 9 3                        ♠ J 7 4
 ♡ A Q J 5 4        N         ♡ 10 3 2
 ◇ 10 5        W        E     ◇ Q 8 3 2
 ♣ Q 8 5 2          S         ♣ A K 10
              ♠ K 10 6 5
              ♡ 7 6
              ◇ K 9 7 6 4
              ♣ 9 3
```

As you can see, you reach a nice little 4-4 fit and rake in eight or nine tricks. But weren't you just lucky? What if opener didn't happen to have four spades? The answer is that you still would have found a playable contract. Let's rearrange North's cards somewhat so that these would be the combined hands:

♠ A J
♡ K 9 8
◇ A Q 8 2
♣ J 7 6 4

♠ K 10 6 5
♡ 7 6
◇ K 9 7 6 4
♣ 9 3

The bidding then would have gone along these lines:

West	North	East	South
pass	1NT	pass	pass
2♡	pass	pass	2♠
pass	2NT	pass	3◇
all pass			

Knowing that spades are only a 4-2 fit, North bids 2NT and South removes to 3◇, showing his other suit.

This is an example of an auction that you aren't likely to have discussed beforehand with partner. However, logical thinking should enable him to figure out what you are apt to have, particularly in light of the fact that you didn't transfer to spades in the first place.